SELECTIONS

FROM THE

HISTORICAL RECORDS

OF THE

HEREDITARY MINISTER OF BARODA

CONSISTING OF

LETTERS FROM BOMBAY, BARODA, POONA AND SATARA GOVERNMENTS

SELECTIONS

FROM THE

HISTORICAL RECORDS

OF THE

HEREDITARY MINISTER OF BARODA

CONSISTING OF

LETTERS FROM BOMBAY, BARODA, POONA AND SATARA GOVERNMENTS

B.A. GUPTE

GYAN

Published by

Gyan Publishing House
5, Ansari Road
Daryaganj, New Delhi-110002
Phone: 011-47034999, 9811692060
E-mail: books@gyanbooks.com

Distribution Network
gyanbooks.com
India, USA, Canada, UK, Australia

ISBN: 978-93-6920-739-8 (HB)
First Published, 1922

2nd Impression 2025

Printed at: Gyan Press, Delhi.

SELECTIONS FROM THE HISTORICAL RECORDS OF THE HEREDITARY MINISTER OF BARODA CONSISTING OF LETTERS FROM BOMBAY, BARODA, POONA AND SATARA GOVERNMENTS
Author: B.A. GUPTE

SELECTIONS FROM THE HISTORICAL RECORDS

OF THE

HEREDITARY MINISTER OF BARODA

SELECTIONS

FROM THE

HISTORICAL RECORDS

OF THE

HEREDITARY MINISTER OF BARODA

CONSISTING OF

LETTERS FROM BOMBAY, BARODA, POONA AND SATARA GOVERNMENTS

COLLECTED BY

RAI BAHADUR B. A. GUPTE, F.Z.S., M.R.S.A.

MEMBER, INDIAN HISTORICAL RECORDS COMMISSION, ETC., LECTURER ON ANCIENT INDIAN HISTORY, AND ETHNOLOGY, CALCUTTA UNIVERSITY

PUBLISHED BY THE

UNIVERSITY OF CALCUTTA

1922

INTRODUCTION

I obtained these 54 original Marathi documents from the hereditary Ministers' family at Baroda. Of these 9 throw a sidelight on the transactions of the Hon'ble East India Company's Officers, 18 of them offer glimpses of the Baroda administration, 6 bespeak of the Poona politics in the last stage of the Maratha Empire, 13 of them are connected with the working of the almost nominal sway of the Raja of Satara, and 8 are chronicles of the times recorded by contemporary Hindi historians in the service of the Divān family. The last group contained a few instances of local miracles and supernatural events. I have omitted them. They are also tainted with evident personal eulogies. The remaining 46 present official transactions and are but the records of actual facts specially important.

I have added annotations containing references to the events recorded in these documents. They show contemporary opinions published by other historians of the Marathas.

The reliable nature of the promises and assurances of the British Officers, the questionable practices of Nāna Phadnavis and his colleagues at Poona, the waning influence of the real Raja of Satara, the efforts of British historians in obtaining historical chronicles from the *daftars* of eminent families through enlightened men like Gangādhar Shāstri, and the real source of Grant Duff's monumental History of the Marathas, are all in evidence in these pages.

It is hoped that these researches in the historical branch of the Council of Post-Graduate Studies of the Calcutta University will prove of some use to future students and historians.

B. A. GUPTE

CONTENTS

LIST OF ILLUSTRATIONS

DOCUMENTS

FROM THE HEREDITARY MINISTERS' FAMILY AT BARODA

DOCUMENT No. 1.

(After compliments.) In the service of the Chhatrapati, one Prayāg Anant Fanase, was a very intelligent, capable, eloquent, brave and good penman at the head of the Māvali and Kokani soldiers. He was appointed *Subhedār* of Fort Satara and Fort Parli (*Shake*, 1571). After the death of the Mahārāja (King Shivāji), Aurangzeb went (to the Deccan) for invading Bijapur. At that time he went to Satara, and digging mines under the bastion, known as Manglāi Buruj he filled it up with large leather jars (*Budhaliñ*) with powder and blew it up. It rose high and fell down. Many people were crushed to death under it. The Emperor's battery began to work. A severe battle followed. Many were killed and many others wounded. *Subhedār* Prayāgji fell down. He was buried under the debris. After nightfall, when the firing ceased, *Kārkuns* and soldiers went to find out who were wounded and who had died. They discovered one end of the scarf Prayāgji wore. On removing part of the debris, they heard Prayāgji say that he was alive, and suggested that care be taken in removing heavy stones. When the slabs were removed, it was found that he was not (seriously) hurt. He was thereupon taken to the Mahārāja. Rājāram Mahārāja granted land at Chinchner and Degaum. It is still in the possession of the family. He (Prayāgji) had two wives. The elder one gave birth to a son. He was named Joti Prāyag, alias Appāji. He (Appāji) had four sons. The elder was Gangādhar Appāji. He died without issue. The second was Chimnāji Appāji whose elder son was Sitārām and younger Sakhārām. The third was Bhāskar alias (Appāji), whose son was the celebrated Rāvji Appāji. The fourth was Rakhmāji Appāji alias Bābāji Appāji. All these were the sons of the first wife. Their descendants will be mentioned in due course. The second wife (of Prayāgji) gave birth to four sons. The eldest was Bāburav Prayāg. The second Nārāyan Prayāg, the third Malhār Prayāg, and the fourth Mādhavrāv Prayāg. Thus they were four. Such was the extent of his family by the two wives. While Appāji was carrying on the duties of the *Subhedārship* of Fort Satara, Chimnāji Appāji came to age. Kharsikar and Vāngikar were employed as *Shiledārs* with their own horses. They were both brave and had taken part in many an expedition. At that time (*Shake*, 1689; *Samvat*, 1824) Damāji Gāikwad died at Pattan. Fattesing Rāv had gone to a neighbouring village. He returned as soon as he heard of the demise, and performed obsequies. Govind Rāv (Gāikwād) was in his province. He heard of it. He asked Government (*Sarkār*) to confer on him the *Khillāt* (of the post) while the eldest member of the family Sayāji Rāv Gāikwād had prior claim. He was asked how he could expect it. After receiving this reply, he (Sayāji Rāv) paid twenty-one *lākhs* of rupees as *nazar* and obtained the *Khillāt*. When Fattesing Rāv heard this, he deputed to Poona Bālāji Yamāji to discuss his claim. He arranged for the proper administration of the province of Gujerat, and went personally to Poona. In the meantime Govindrāv paid the *nazar* and distributed the *māmlats* among his own people. He paid rupees twenty *lākhs* out of the promised sum. The officers he had selected, received their *sanads* and went to Gujerat. (But) Fattesing had already arranged for the proper administration of that province. The new officers arrived. They were not allowed to take charge. The treasury stored by Damāji in the vestibule was removed by Govindrāv with the help of an army of 10,000 strong. When Fattesing opened negotiations about the appointment, he was told that as it had been already conferred (on another) it was not advisable to re-open the question. After many importunities Fattesing Rāv was told, (with the object of keeping him contented) that one of the two, should carry on military duties, and the other should carry on the civil duties of the post. Such (he was told) should be the procedure introduced. On this, Damāji applied the *kunkum* (red powder) to the forehead of Gobindrāv's mother. Damajis marriage was postponed owing to some dispute. He married another (meanwhile?). When Damāji's proposal was accepted, he was again married to that woman (?) The firstborn was Fattesing Rāv. Govindrāv was born after him. So each wife had her own son. In this manner, although Govindrāv was younger, as his mother had received the honour of the red powder in the *first* instance, he claimed seniority, because his mother was the senior wife. He, therefore, got the *khillāt*. He coveted the province. But he accepted the service, because he was afraid of losing his seniority. Fattesing

Rāv accepted civil duties. Govindrāv made arrangements for the expenses of the army, obtained permission of the Peshva and went to Baroda. It was settled that he should serve with 3,000 strong. Govindrāv gave in writing to that effect. He was present with the Peshva during the Nijagal(?) and Beder expeditions. The officers he had sent to Gujerat could not receive charge from Fattesing Rāv's *Thānedārs*. There was a battle. In this battle Chimnāji Appāji, Annā Bhāu and Vāngikar were the officers employed under Kharsikar. In the action near Songad, he himself, Chimnāji Appāji and some of Vāngikar's soldiers were killed. After this, Govindrāv complained, through Mahādji Sinde, Māloji Ghorpade and Tāmbekar Nāik, that by granting civil powers to Fattesing he was made to suffer. He, therefore, should have the entire control. He was told in reply by Rāvsāheb Peshva, that there shall be no change in what the *Sarkār* had done. If he repeated the request, it would not be tolerated, and added,

"If you say that you have suffered loss, you should re-open the subject with my consent. You did not listen to this, extravagantly spent money, and created disturbance. The distribution of work was settled with your mutual consent. You and your brother should co-operate and serve the *Sarkār* without any friction. Instead of that you bring disputes to the *Sarkār*. What is this?"

There was then no help. Pātil Bāva (Mahādji Sindia) started for Hindustan (N. India). Govindrāv showed willingness to accompany him, Pātil Bāva said,

"You are in possession of Davadi and Nimbgāv, and if you remain with me I shall grant villages yielding twenty to twenty-five thousand a year, as revenue." In reply (Govindrāv) said "You have secured for me the *Khillāt* and the (*sardārship*) by recommending me to the *Sarkār*. I accept them."

"In this speech I have lost all hope of the position. Govind or said, In my accompanying you and accepting your kind offer, I realize the influence of my Fate. It is better to die or to turn an ascetic. One has to do this or that, but you say that I should accept your offer." Pātil Bāva replied, "Have I spared myself in speaking about you? I spoke strongly in the prescribed manner. But what can I do, when the *Sarkār* commands thus? After I know your wishes, I shall (again) speak in accordance with them and in a way acceptable to (the *Sarkār*)." He (Govindrāv) said, "On your way to Hindustan pray take a turn and go through Gujerat for my sake. And establish my control. If so, I shall accompany you." Then he (Sindia) replied, "There is no objection to go with you. But Fattesing Rāv is in power; because he is the elder, he has obeyed *Sarkār's* orders, and you have accepted military service. He, instead of persisting in claiming the position of the elder, accepted the decision and obeyed orders. He is in possession of the whole estate. You are unable to do anything and therefore you say all this. You ought to have thought of this course before. That you did not do. What is the use of speaking now? I did not desist from working for you. And, therefore, I suggested a way to reconciliation. If you do not like it, what is the remedy?" After he said so, Govindrāv replied, "What I did, was under instructions from you. In future also I shall follow your advice. Whatever you do, pray remember that I am your man. That is my prayer." When he said so, he was told, "You wish me to pass through Gujerat! Very well. The *Sarkār* should pass such an order. I shall ask the *Sarkār* and act accordingly."

Shrimant (The Peshva) gave (Mahādji) permission to go to Hindusthan. When begging leave he asked for permission to go through Gujerat and to pass through the Broach District *viâ* Pāyagad and Malva. "On my way I shall settle my dispute with Fattesing Rāv Gāikvād about the Vaghod District. Govind Rāv Gāikvād says that he would accompany me. I shall consult him on the subject and obey (your) orders." He was thereupon commanded to settle his own *mahāl* (tract). Vaghod District had been handed over to him (Fattesing) on behalf of the *Sarkār*. Such was the order. Patil Bāva then asked Govindrāv to accompany him. Govindrāv spoke of what thus happened (to Khando Āvji) and added that he had to prepare himself to go. "Think of this," he (Khando Avji) said, "As you have to go to a very distant place, keep a suitable retinue. It should be in proportion to your reputation. You have already told him (Mahādji) that you will arrange for funds. What is to be done now?" He (Govindrāv) said, "I shall take Pātil Bāva to Gujerat. With his help I wish to establish my power. If I incur debts, I shall repay them. Do I wish to avoid repayment of anybody's dues? You can arrange this. Then why ask me?" After this, Khandoba sent for Rāvji Appāji and spoke to him (about the matter). He said (Govindrāv) wishes to go. He has a powerful ally. It is not nice to advise him (Govindrāv) to ask him (Sindia) to advance the sum. If any financial difficulty arises on the way, the result will depend on what he pays. On reaching Gujerat, we reach our own *maḥāls* (tracts). We can borrow a few rupees, but this is a wretched state and, therefore, I cannot make up my mind to start. Arrange the matter as you conveniently can. I shall settle the payment through you—either here (at Poona) or there (in Gujerat). But this (business) must be accomplished." On this Rāvba (Rāvji Appāji) told some merchants that

Govindrāv (Gāikwād) was going with Sindia (Mahādji). "Your business is to supply clothes and accoutrements. See if you can do this" (in this case). When he said so, the dealers immediately supplied it (all). When they asked for payment, they were told, "It would be done, when the usual amount is received from the *Sarkār*." Khandoba suggested that "After everything is ready, your work would be done through Bālāji." On his saying so, the Nāik promised to advance fifty thousand rupees.

When he (Khandoba) was asked for payment, he replied, "He (Govindrāv) was going with Pātil Bāva through Gujerat, where he would establish his power. The *Sarkār* has decided that they should pass through Mālva (as well). When they go there, we shall pay you." The Nāik had already heard of the Pātil Bāva's departure (such respectable people would not tell lies). He, therefore, promised to advance the sum, "but," he added, "Rāvba should admit his responsibility. Then I shall pay." Pātil Bāva, therefore, took Rāvba to him (Nāik) and related what Pātil Bāva spoke to the *Shrimant*. He (Nāik) said, 'If you stand security, I shall advance the amount." Rāvba told (him) aside, "I have my say. They are *Sardārs*, I am poor. What is the value of my credit in between? You turn towards me (as trustworthy). How can I tell you to put obstacles, in their work? You are influential. You are (Nāik) related to *Sarkār*. I cannot realize that your money will not be paid. After this (explanation) do as you please." Bhide (Nāik) said, "I am not going to catch you (by the throat) Say—'Yes'—in their presence." After they (Rāvji and Bhide) spoke in the presence of both (Pātil Bāva and Govindrāv) and Rāvba stood security. He then took a promissory note, but added that he did not quite rely on the document alone. "I shall have to recover the amount from you. If you agree I shall pay, if not, I shall not." Rāvba thereupon looked at (the face of) Khandoba. He (Khandoba) said, "Why are you afraid? Say—yes! When we have a master like Pātil Bāva, what is the value of this sum (against that)?" At this time he (Rāvba) said, "Yes,—Pay." The Nāik then caused the amount to be paid. In this manner he (Rāvba) influenced many merchants and dealers, and secured millions of rupees. Rāvba used to go to Govindrāv and speak to him on other subjects, but to monetary transactions Khandoba when alone refused to refer in his conversation. Rāvba never spoke of it himself. After making these arrangements, it was decided, at the time of starting (on the expedition), that a *kārkun* be engaged on behalf of the creditor. Govindrāv (himself) suggested, "As Rāvba stands security, let him go with me. I shall then repay through him." It met with Bhide's approval. (Govindrāv) said "This (arrangement) will facilitate the settlement of my transactions and save your credit." Rāvba replied, "Have I no elders at home? If I go with you, who is to pay my expenses and to support the family? I have been working here with the *Darbār*. If I go out and return after a long interval, I shall have to begin life again. What is the advantage? Take a *Kārkun*. It will be all right." On this, Bābāsāheb (Gāikwād) and the Nāik (money-lender) decided that Rāvba should himself go. They said, "We shall take care of you as suggested in your remark." When both of them pressed the point, Rāvba had no alternative. At this time all creditors who had supplied articles also suggested that, if Rāvba were to go, he would carefully arrange for the repayment. "We feel confident on this," Rāvba replied, "you all wish me to go. It is all very well, but all payments are to be made through Khandoba. If the amounts are not paid, you will accuse me of *mis-appropriation.* I do not aspire to such a *reputation.*" They said, "You take interest in our business and, therefore, you will by all means recover the amount. If it is not realized, it would be our misfortune. We shall not blame you." In this manner all the creditors settled the deputation of Rāvba. Govindrāv repeated the offer. Khandoba also said the same thing. Rāvba, therefore prepared to go. Rāvba thereupon took Gopālrav Bhide Nāik to Nāna (Fadnavis) who said, "I have had transactions with the *Sarkār*. Kindly permit Rāvba to go with him for a few days to facilitate repayment." Nāna said, "If he is useful to you, I shall look after his duties here." Rāvba bowed and said, "I spoke to the Nāik in several ways but he insists on my going. I then told him,—I cannot go without Nāna's permission. He has, therefore, brought me here to obtain that permission. When you order me to go I have no alternative. I am going, until this work is done in a few days. All this reflects the lustre of your self. If I am able to retain my fidelity, I shall be able to accomplish this work. Should I keep you informed of it?" He (Nāna) said, "No." Rāvba thus accompanied Govindrāv. He had access to Pātil Bāva and to all others (officers). Everybody liked him.

At this stage, it was found very difficult to go *viâ* Nāsik and through the Bassein District. When Fattesing learnt that Pātil Bāva was going through Songad and Dharampur with Govindrāv (Gāikwād) he collected all *rājas, raises, merāts,* dacoits, Bhils, Kolis, Rānas, Thākurdās, gave them assurances (?), gave them entertainments, dresses, and told them in a respectful manner to defeat the enemy (Govindrāv) so as to prevent their reaching Baroda. "There lies" (he added) "the test of your valonr. This will be the recompense for the protection we gave you. If not" (he added firmly) "I will take back from you every lane and alley. Be sure." When he said so people, who were naturally eager to do mischief were rather glad. It was a dangerous thing to travel alone. Horses laden with stores were likely to be lost. Unwary horsemen were likely to lose their ponies. Pedestrians lost their clothes. They were tied to trees. Whenever people halted (for rest) they lost their horses and belongings. Such was the trouble created. Sindia (Mahādji) was obliged to keep in all directions spies, guards, piquets and vanguards even two hours before sunset. He felt that he would not have suffered in this manner if he had not taken Govindrāv with him "God's will be done" (he exclaimed). In this manner he anyhow crossed the Narbada with great difficulty. Under fear of danger to life in going to Baroda, they left Cambay to the left and Petlavad to the right, and went to Pāyagad *viâ* Dākur. During these troubles Rāvba was consulted and he tendered valuable advice. His lucky stars removed all obstacles. There was no one who could stand security for payments required in the army. Hundreds of men and animals had to be fed. Three or four times did Rāvba remind Govindrāv and Khandoba that they said (at Poona) that there would be no want of money as soon as they reached their territory (and added) "Make some arrangement for the repayment of the previous debt." Khandopant replied, "Rāvba, you see all that happens. We are not speaking with you with reserve. What is the remedy to the question you raise? If there were any neglect (on our part) in obtaining funds your remark would have been appropriate." Rāvba replied, "They will ask *me* when they demand repayment, I have to keep them (creditors) informed. You will also blame me for writing (to them) without your consent. Or they will accuse me of co-operation through corrupt motives. I am helpless as I have to obey both sides. I am therefore obliged to fit up matters in a suitable manner." On this Govindrāv said, "Rāvba, Khandoba told me the purport of your conversation. I see and hear myself (all that is happening). If we go to Gujerat to take possession of the *mahāls* from him (Fattesing) we are not sure whether we shall reach our destination or (nobody knows) what may happen. If we declare open war with him, he has formed a treaty with the *Sarkār*. We have no permission to interfere with it (the treaty). If I were to threaten them (local officers), we have diverted our route through his fear. How can therefore we speak to them (the officers). Tell me. We ought not to have left Poona. But you have brought us out by helping the preparation. I shall not forget your obligations. Your brother laid his life for me in the battle of Songad. I know it. I am indebted to you in every way. May Hari (God) bring the day on which I shall be able to repay (these obligations). You alone can help to bring it about. Nobody else can do it. Do not be anxious about the repayment (of the debt). I will get the whole thing done through you. Be assured." He said so. When Sindia came to Pāyagad on his way to Hindustan, somebody told Pātil Bāva "all Kolis, Mewāts, Thākurs and Princes have been commanded by Fattesing to annoy Pātil Bāva. Do not allow him to pass safely. Our own Mevāts and Kolis are therefore no longer ours. They will come in our way. The Gāikwād (Fattesing) is the master of the place. They will not disobey him. They will sacrifice their lives, in doing their duty. Such is the state (here). We should therefore start (from here) after making some arrangement about this state of things." On enquiry, it was found to be too true. Being thus sure that his army will not be able to pass safely through this route, he (Pātil Bāva) sent for the Thākur of Bāria and told him "We have to start (now). Make arrangements on our way and help us to go to Ujjain." He replied, "You are my master. I take up the responsibility of safe conduct through my tract. What can I say about further progress?" His territory extended over 20 to 25 miles. He conducted the army safely. To prevent trouble with the Kolis, he distributed dresses and other presents among them and told them (Sindiā and Gāikwād) to do the same as far as Kushalgad. They agreed. On reaching Dabod, the Thākur of Kushalgad was sent for and offering many assurances he was asked to conduct the army to Ujjain. He (the Thākur) said that the Rāja was living in the fort and that he would go and give him this message. (He added) "After his visit we shall obey your orders and serve you." They then went to Kushalgad. On nearing Ujjain, Rāvba said to Govindrāv and Khandopant, "It is now three or four months since I left (Poona). Pray give me permission to go back. I am going. You settle the payment of the debt in the best way you like. In Poona they will give me no rest. Kindly remember this and then do what you like." Khandopant replied, "You see and know everything here. What am I to add? You propose going back. I will consult the Mahārāja and let you know." The Mahārāja was there. He (turned to him) and asked him (what to do). The Mahārāja (Gāikwād) said "Rāvba! I brought you because I trust you. Pātil Bāva could not help and therefore he was obliged to abandon the original route. Although you know this, you express your desire to go back. But stay for a few days and (let us see) if we can feel our way (out of this difficulty). Otherwise (it seems) our end has approached. After getting out of this affair, that will be the real way which God Shri Hari will find out (for us). Rāvba, you say you are going back. Does it become you (to say so)?" He then passed his hand round Rāvba's neck and added, "My own brother has made me go from door to door. You must have (in previous birth) been heavily indebted to me (* * *). I have no confidence in anybody else. You have already accomplished a task which Khandoba could not. You have saved my credit. Khandoba gave me timely information (it is true). Still I am much indebted to you. May God relieve me out of this debt (* *) for which I am so much obliged to you. I am conscious of it." At this speech (Rāvba) was obliged to change his mind and to stay with him (Govindrāv). Where Khandoba could not help, Rāvba accomplished his work. All men (in the camp) were inclined to listen to and act up to his advice. They were about to proceed to Gwalior, but the news of the death of Peshva Rāvsāheb Mādhavrāv Ballāl reached the camp. (He expired on *San sattas Arbainal, Kārtik.*) Ramābāi sāheb went a *Sati* (burnt herself on his pyre). Everybody was sorry. His senior (elder) was Raghoba Dāda and his heir was Nārāyanrāv Ballāl. He was taken to Satara. He took his *khillāt* in *Shake* 1695. He conducted the duties for nine months.

On the day which was the combined 13th and 14th of the first half of *Bhādrapad* (*Arba*) Sumersing Gārdi conspired with Dādāsāheb, accepted the offer of money, and received from him a written order. In the *Wāda* situated in the Shanwār Peth, while they both (uncle and nephew) were living under the same roof (Sumersing) forced his way into it and killed Nārāyan Rāv sāheb. Subsequently Dādāsāheb invaded the country of the Nizam with the army. This was the information received by Pātil Bāva.

After this it was settled through Krishna Rāv Ballāl that a *jahāgir* of twenty *lākhs* (a year) be accepted from the Mongals, and Nawab Rukam Daula and Nizam-ul-Mulk went to see Dādāsāheb. After some friendly negotiation the *jahāgir* so accepted was returned. On hearing this Nāna (Fadnis) informed Pātil Bāva that Nārāyan Rāv Peshwa's wife Gangābāi was in the family way. Dādāsāheb will treacherously do her harm. "I am taking her to Fort Purandar. Because people will say that we brought some outsider (child) and declare it as Nārāyan Rāv's. There should therefore be some witness at the accouchement. She should be an elderly (woman). That is why she is carried there (to Purandar). Come back immediately with your army." Such was the letter. Pātil Bāva therefore turned back. In the Desh, Shahāji Bhosle of Akalkot had raised a revolt. Dādāsāheb thereat deputed Trimbakrāv *māmā*. The Nāgpur Bhosle was mixed up (in the revolt). Nāna induced him to be friendly. When the news of the birth of Nārāyan Rāv's son was received, the Mongal, and the *Māma*, joined together and conspired against Dādāsāheb with the consent of Sakhāram Pant Bāpu, Moroba Dāda, Bābuji Naik, and Krishnarāv Ballāl. When Dādāsāheb learnt this, he directed his steps (to Poona), and attacked *Māma* and the Mongals. *Māma* was defeated. Dādāsāheb captured him. The soldiers turned their backs. At this juncture Hari Pant Tātia, showed great rectitude, called all *sardārs*, gave them assurances, mobilized them again, saw the Nawāb at Shahajira, gave him encouragement, and secured diplomacy.

Mādhavrāv Nārāyan was born on Monday the 7th[1] of the first half of *Vaishākh Shake* 1696 (*Jaya Samvatsar*).

[1] It was on the 18th of April, 1774 (Grant Duff Vol. II, p. 264).

People were delighted. They distributed sugar. Rejoicings were held in every house All *saṃsthāniks*, *sardārs*, and foreign rulers and their *Amirs* learnt of it. They were delighted. Dādāsāheb was taken to Purandar. He met Hari Pant Tātia and the Nawāb. When they joined him he crossed the Narbada. To reconcile Dādāsāheb, Sakhārām Bāpu and Nāna followed him up to Verul. Dādāsāheb grew suspicious, and turned towards Gujerat. On his way (his wife) Anandi Bāi gave birth to a son at Dhar. Bājirāv II was born with his face down (towards the earth).[1] He stayed there for a few days and desired to go to Surat through Gujerat. Pātil Bāva went to Poona according to Nānā's letter. Dādāsāheb was accompanied by an army and some *Mānkaris*. He sent for Govind Khanderāv Chitnis (of Satara) and asked him whether he had friendly relations with Nānā. Govindrāv Chitnis replied, "The Mahārāja (of Satara) would not destroy what he himself had done." "If that is the case" (said Dādāsāheb) "how am I to induce the *Huzur Mānkaris* and *Sardārs* to join me?" He replied, "I and all the servants of the Mahārāja will never disobey his orders. They can be called together only on receiving letters from the *Huzur*. They will come at the sight of his letters. There is no doubt about that."

At this suggestion, it was settled that such letters should be written. Letters with proper titles recognized by the Mahārāja, were addressed (as if written by his command) and Sadāshiv Rāv Laxman Chitnis was deputed (to Satara) to get them attested. He went to Satara, got the letters, completed (signed) by *Shrimant* Rājārām Sāheb Mahārāja and handed them, over to the head of the messengers (*Jāsuds*). They were despatched under

[1] This is a bad omen.

the stringent orders of Nāna. They went as far as Dhar, handed the letters over to the *Samsthāniks*,—officers of the Cavalry and Infantry. Those who got the letters, quietly started with their followers without consulting anybody else. In this manner all the people who were with Dādāsāheb returned (to Poona). With him there remained his personal staff, bodyguards, two or three companies of State Cavalry, two or three thousand soldiers of the infantry and Sakhāram Hari (Gupte) the head of the *Kārkuns* of the "vegetable" Department. Subsequently he rose after the death of Nārāyan Rāv. He was (formerly) the manager of Anandi Bāi. He was the *Bakshi* (a General in the Army). All left (Dhar). He was a favourite of (Dādāsāheb) because he was doubly connected as an officer (of two Departments). He was a brave man (*Talvār Bahāddar*). He proved his valour in two or three expeditions. A soldier and a penman combined and a great administrator in addition. Dādāsāheb wished to form an alliance with the British and to be the sole ruler (at Poona). At this juncture, the main army deserted him. He remained alone with four or five thousand soldiers. He (Dādāsāheb) intended going to Cape Comorin at the head of the army he expected from Surat. On the other hand, while Pātil Bāva was going to Desh, Khando Avji of Tāmbegāv was taken very ill. It was a rapid march. He (Khando) suffered much. When he found that his case was hopeless he said to Govindrāv (Gāikwād), "I pulled on during the last ten or twelve years on the strength of Rāvji's fidelity. Wherever there was any difficulty, I told him that he alone could get out of it, and did work at the risk of his life. His elder brother Chimnāji Appāji sacrificed his life at the battle of Songad. I have therefore promised to him that I will arrange for hereditary grants to him. He has similarly worked loyally with you, preserving amiable relation with the *Darakdārs* and with the ladies in your household. They always trusted him. He must be kept above want. He was given two or three important duties. They paid him for his expenses. The usual *nazar* and *Darbār*-charges were recovered from him. He is acquainted and is friendly with everybody. Everybody wants Rāvba. He would do no harm to anybody. He was therefore a great favourite. You asked him to undertake all preparations for the expedition. Although you had no cash, he obtained it from Bhide. He also got materials (on credit) from the Boharas, cloth merchants, Gosāvis, and Jingars, all worth *lākhs* of Rupees. The limit (of repayment) has expired. He accompanied you. What shall I tell him if he asks me (about provision for himself)? When you gave orders, he never uttered a word (in hesitation). It is not possible to get such a man even after a great search. But there was a lucky coincidence like the proverb, "God sent water at the time of sacred ablutions." Thus were preparations for the expedition accomplished. I am dying. Had I lived, it was my intention to go to Gujerat and salute you seated on the *masnad*. But God does not like it. What to do? Cannot survive. If Rāvba gets into difficulties, do as you like and do not allow any troubles to overtake him. If he remains free (to act) he will save you in a thousand ways, and save himself (too). Nāna (Fadnis), Haripant, Sakhārām Bāpu, Moroba Dāda Pānse, Khāsgivāle, and Rām Shāstri are all friendly with him. I alone know how I induced him to accompany you. You also know it partly. Therefore if you take him as your right hand man, your *Sardārship* will be thoroughly organised by all means. No other man can do that. Be assured of this." Such is the way in which he spoke to Govindrāv. He then became unconscious. He could not speak. Finding him at the point of death, Govindrāv left his bed-side. He was very sorry. He knew that he had to establish his *Sardārship* by alternate fasting and food-taking. He was sure of the confidence Rāvba commanded. When he left Poona, the creditors hoped from day to day, to obtain refunds. But they waited in vain. On his reaching destination, they made a row. They surrounded Khandoba. For two or three days they remained round him. There was no payment. They therefore thought of surrounding Govindrāv's tent. Khandoba got an inkling. He placed guards and piquets round the tent, and quietly arranged that no one was allowed to go inside (the tent). Some people rose to enter the tent. They were stopped. Khandoba said, "I am present on the spot. I do not refuse to repay. You will be paid in full. Why do you go to the Chief? If you disrespect him in this manner you will get nothing. If you remain quiet, you will be the gainers." He said so. At this moment Rāvba arrived. When he saw that Khando Āvji was surrounded (by creditors and their agents) he walked towards Govindrāv's tent. There also he saw a crowd. Then.........

(This document seems to have been written by a close associate and left unfinished through death or otherwise.)

DOCUMENT No. 2.

To

Akhandit Laxmi Alankrit Rājmanya Rājashri Antāji Prayāg *Nāmjād*, Khālsa, Taluka, Kudāl Medhe, District Parali.

After compliments. From Fattesing Bhosle.

Dated *Suru san Asharir maya va allaf.*

Kalambe, Taluka Parali, is a town, an *inām* granted to Prayāgji Anant *Subhedār* of Fort Satara. Its annual *Khālsa* revenue amounts to Rs. 240. Of these Rs. 100 have been fixed as State revenue. Recover annually this sum of Rs. 100. The balance of Rs. 140 should be written off in the name of the said person. Do not demand the production of the *sanad* from year to year. Recover only the State Revenue according to agreement. The rest of the amount should be written off. Know this, 10th Moon of the *Jilkād* month.

(Seal.)

DOCUMENT No. 3.

(Seal.)

Ordered (addressed to) *Rājashri Pant* Pradhān in charge of town Kalambe, Taluka Parali on *Suma, Saba Shitani va allaf.*

Rājashri Joti Anant is being paid (in the place of *Sardesh-mukhi*) the sum of Rs. 30 a year for the worship of *Shri* Yavateshvar of the said town. This is sanctioned. Therefore you should annually pay this sum. If last year's balance is still due, that also should be paid. Know this. 28th Moon (of the month of) *Safar*. True order. ...

(Seal.)

DOCUMENT No. 4.

(Seal.)

To

Rājashri Gangādhar Joti and Sitārām Chimnāji *Yabin* Joti Anant and Bhāskar Joti and Chimnāji Joti.

From

Mādhavrāv Nārāyan Pradhān (written on) *Asiyasar Suma Araba Tisain, maya va allaf*, Shake 1716, *Samvatsar* named Anand.

You came to Poona to *Huzur* (to me) and prayed that your grandfather Prayāg Anant received from Shrimant late Shāhu Maharaja Chhatrapati, the village of Kalambe of the Wāi District, as an *inām* (freehold) including all sources of revenue of all legal rites and granted Royal *sanads*. These *sanads* were in your house but were burnt. Therefore you got fresh *sanads* from *Shrimant* Tārābāi Sāheb and Rājārām Mahārāja Chhatrapati *Swāmi*. But the District cess, and the five acres of land from Parashurām Pandit Pratinidhi have been granted (as *inām*) to Antāji Vāsudev. And the *Khālsa and Sardesh-mukhi* cess are being credited to the state. You are in the enjoyment of merely the *mokāsa* cess. All the descendants of your great grandfather Prayāgji Anant are not alive this day. To the survivors, (you beg) I should grant the *zilla* cess and the said land from the Pratinidhi. The annual revenue (of this land) amounts to Rs. 350. He may be granted in exchange land of equal value, and the *zilla* cess and land revenue may be granted *inām* to you and fresh orders be issued for your enjoyment thereof. In consideration of this request, and finding that the entire village of Kalambe of Taluka Parali District Wāi has been registered in the *inām* grants of the state. But that you are in enjoyment of only the *mokāsa* cess. The *inām* grant is not continued.

As you have been loyally serving the state for a long time, it is incumbent (on the state) to make sufficient provision for you, it has been decided as a favour, that excluding the *khālsa* and *Sardeshmukhi*, and state garden, the District cess (be granted to you). The land belonging to *Rājashri* Parashurām Pandit Pratinidhi and given in *inām* to Anāji Vāsudev yields Rs. 350 a year. In exchange of Rs. 350 out of village Sare, *Tāluka* Haveli District Karād shall be granted to him. The District cess and the land and the *one third inām* cess are (hereby) granted to you. Including the entire *Kulbābs* and *Kulkānus*, present dues, future dues. Moreover you are appointed the rightful *Kalurin ināmdār* from this year by a new grant from the Sarkār. (You should) therefore consider the District cess and the land as *inām* unto you and your descendants. Enjoy it as an *inām* and be happy. Know this. Second Moon of the month of *Srāvan*. Such is the order.

(Seal.)

DOCUMENT No. 5.

(May peace prevail)

Order of freehold (*ināmpatra*) granted to *Rājashri* Joti Anant Prabhu by *Shri* Rājārām Chhatrapati *Swāmi*.

You came to the *Huzur* at Fort Satara near Shahunagar, and said that the Mahārāja *Swāmi* granted to your grandfather Prayāg Anant, the village of Kalambe *tāluka* Parali, *prānt* Satara, including the *Swarāj* and *Monglāi*, rites, the one-third due of the *inām*, all taxes and all cesses, the present and future revenue, ownership over the water, grass, wood, stones and other minerals, etc. That he was made the hereditary rightful *ināmdār* and was favoured with the necessary letters. After this your grandfather died and the late Mahārāja granted the same village to your father Antāji Prayāg with hereditary rites. While in the enjoyment of these grants in the said village, you had a house in which all the documents were kept. That house took fire which destroyed all the property, including the said documents. You informed the late Dowager Mother (Tārābāi) of this (mishap.) She kindly granted again fresh documents on 29th Moon or *Rajāb Suru San Sālas Khānsāni.* That you have been enjoying those privileges. Your father Antāji Prayāg died and requested that fresh documents be granted and he showed (to the *Huzur*) the letters granted by the late Queen-Mother. Taking them into consideration and the fact that you are old loyal 'servants' of the state, it is incumbent to support you. The *Swāmi* (king) was therefore graciously pleased to grant to your grandfather Prayāg Anant the *sanad* of the said village including Mongul and *Swarāj* (our

Government) dues on either side, including (*khālsa*) the grant of the one-third cess and local taxes including all customary taxes, balance of dues and future dues, (grant) ownership over the water, the trees, grass, wood, minerals, buried treasures and deposits. Papers (orders) were thus given. While in the enjoyment of the said grant, your grandfather died. After that, the late Mahārāja granted similar papers (*sanad*) to your father Antāji Prayāg. While still in the enjoyment of the said grant your hereditary *wāda* (house) was destroyed by fire. In it, all papers and things were reduced to ashes. Among them were the papers (*sanads*). On that account the Queen-Mother gave you fresh *sanads* for hereditary enjoyment. You are in enjoyment in accordance therewith. Your father Antāji Prayāg (also) died. Hereby the said village is (again) granted to you (*on similar terms repeated*) as a hereditary *inām*. You should therefore enjoy as a hereditary grant the said village of which boundary has been marked.

Compared	I agree	I agree	I agree
	Sumant	*Mantri*	*Sarkār*
			(King)

Dated 22nd *Jilkād Suma Arba Shitani māyātain va allaf.*

DOCUMENT No. 6.

Order—(addressed to All Officers concerned from) *Rājeshri* Pant Pradhān down to the officer in charge, Village Kalambe, *Taluka* Parali *Prānt* Wāi (dated) *Suma Saba Mayā va allaf.*

The *Khālsa* cess of the said village (granted to) *Rājeshri* Baburāv Krishna as sub-grant of the Fort of Satara, and (excluding *Sardeshmukhi* cess) the cash allotment assigned to *Shri* Yavateshwar, and the duty of collecting the revenue of the private garden (of the king) assigned to *Rājeshri* Nāvji Shankar Haibatrāv. These have been (hereby) resumed and from this year forward they have been assigned to *Rajeshri* Joti Anant *Subhedār*, late Governor of the Fort of Satara who has been enjoying a hereditary stipend from Satara. This order should therefore be registered and excluding the grant of Rs. 30 a year, the balance of the three items (taken together) should be regularly paid to him as a stipend in exchange. Know this. Dated 11th Moon of *Safar*. Positive order.

(Seal.)

REGISTERED.

Azam Bhāskar Rāv Vithal wrote (for a copy) on the 10th Moon of *Savant* 1909. Bajāba Bāpuji Kārkun compared it with the original and it has been attested as a true copy on the 28th of April, 1853 at the Residency of Baroda.

(*English signature.*)

DOCUMENT No. 7.

(Seal.)

Budget of grants promised in lieu of the salaries of the old (infirm) and deceased *Kārkuns* of the late King of Satara—dated *Surusan Ihide ashār mayātain va allaf.*

	Cash payment.	Annual grants in *Hons*.		Monthly grant.
1	1400	21	(To)	Sitārām Bhāskar. *Subhedar* Gangādhar Joti has become old. He has no son. His brother Bhāskar Joti is dead, therefore his nephew gets a perpetual grant of 1800 *Hons*; out of this a monthly grant Rs. 21. He is 35 years of age.
1	200	3	(To)	*Kārkun* Nārāyan Sitārām. Chimnāji Joti is dead, therefore in his place his grandson to be paid out of the perpetual grant of 200 *Hons* cash allowance.

Total two persons. Among them the total annual allowance for employing retainers, Rs. 24 per month sanctioned from the beginning according to practice. Know this—4th Moon *Jamādilāval.*

(Seal.)

Compared by Bajya Bāpuji *Kārkun.*

In order to obtain countersignature on this account *Ajam* Bhāskar Rāv Vithal sent a letter dated 10th Moon of *Chaitra Samvat* 1909. Thereupon the original in existence was compared with this one and a duly signed true copy is hereby granted on 28th April, 1853, from the Baroda Residency.

(*English Officer's signature.*)

DOCUMENT No. 8.

(Seal.)

Shrimant Mahārāj (Dowager) Mother granted an *inām-patra* (*sanad*) to Antāji Prayāg Prabhu that you came to the *Huzur* at Satara, prayed that viilage Kalambe, *Tāluka* Parali *Prānt* Satara, was granted (as *inām*) to your father Prayāgji Anant, that it included the rights enjoyed by the local as well as Moghal administrations

(terms similar to the former document are repeated here).

DOCUMENT No. 9.

To

Rājeshri Gangādhar Joti and Sitārām Chimnāji *bin* Joti Anant and Bhāskar Joti and Rakhmāji Joti.

From

Mādhavrāv Nārāyan Pradhān (writes on) *Asikhad Suma Arba tisain mayā va allaf. Shake* 1716, of the *Anand Samvatsara.*

You came to the *Huzur* at Poona and prayed that your great grand-father Anant, was favoured by the late Shrimant Shāhu Mahārāja Chhatrapati, with the *inām* of the village of Kalambe, etc., (repetition of the terms mentioned above) 2nd Moon *Savāl.*

(Seal.)

DOCUMENT No. 10.

By order of the Pant Pradhān.

Written on *Suma, saba, sabāni, mayā, va allaf.* The *Sardeshmukhi*, etc., cess of the village of Kalambe is in the enjoyment of Bhavāni Shankar Haibatrāv. It should be discontinued and transferred to Joti Anant late *Subhedar's* account, etc.

11th Moon *Safar.*

(Seal.)

DOCUMENT No. 11.

(Chhatrapati
Rāja Shahu's
Seal.)

To

Pant Pradhān and all officers concerned with the village of Kalambe (repetition) were in the enjoyment of the late Joti Anant *Subhedār*. After his death, the said village is hereby granted to his son Gangādhar Joti, etc. (repetition) 21st Moon *Moharam*.

(Seal.)

DOCUMENT No. 12.

(Chhatrapati
Raja Shāhu's
Seal.)

To

Pant Pradhān and all officers concerned.

The village of Kalambe is in the possession and enjoyment of Gangādhar Joti *Subhedār*. He has become old, it is hereby transferred to Sitārām Bhāskar his nephew (repetitions of the detailed terms.) 4th Moon *Rabiulāval*.

(Seal.)

DOCUMENT No. 13.

To

A. L. A. R. R. Mahādji Keshav

From

Mādhavrāv Nārāyan Pradhān

Written on *Suma Saba Sabain mayā va allaf.*

The grant of the *sardeshmukhi* cess of village Kalambe which has been withdrawn from you and has been granted to the late *Subhedār* of Satara—Joti Anant, from this year forward as a hereditary stipend—an item out of the Satara budget. In the face of these facts the *Huzur* is informed that you do not straightforwardly pay him the amount. You are therefore hereby directed to pay unhesitatingly the said sum in accordance with the *Sanad.* You need not feel depressed, but there should in future be no complaint about this matter. Know this. 2nd Moon *Rabilākhar.* True order.

(Seal.)

DOCUMENT No, 14.

To

A. L. A. R. R. Gangādhar Joti, late *Subhedār*

Fort Satara

From

Mādhavrāv Nārāyan Pradhān

Dated *Suru, san, Khamas Tisain mayā va allaf.*

For your domestic expenses 25,000 bundles of grass have been granted out of village Akle, *Tāluka* Satara in accordance with the *sanad*, granted in the name of Krishnāji Anant.

Thus :—bundles about,

10,000 (to be supplied) on the 1st Moon of *Saval, san ihide Tisain*

15,000 on the 27th Moon of *Jamādilākhar san arbā Tisain*

Total 25,000 bundles of grass have been granted to you. Therefore a grass-land yielding the said 25,000 bundles has (hereby) been assigned to you (of which) the boundaries are :—

To the east (lies) the piece of land granted to Krishnāji Jagannāth of the Dhāvadsi state as *Chamhārpenda*, to the west (lies) the stone near the stream which runs down from the top of the Meruling hill. Below that, lies the fringe of cactus at the corner, below that (lies) the stream, below that (stands to the east of the stream) the *diospyros* tree (*tembi*). The jungle so described has (hereby) been granted to you. You should therefore get the grass-land guarded every year and cut the grass. Enquiry was made for two or three years about the yield of the said grass-land through a *kārkun* specially deputed. (It is ascertained) that it amounts to less than 25,000 bundles. If it yields more, you should send it to the *Sarkār*. Know this. 7th Moon *Rajjab* (in the presence of the *Huzur*). End. Registered.

DOCUMENT No. 15.

Rājarām
Narapati
Harshanidān
Mādhavrāv Ballāl
Mukhya Pradhān

To

Pant Pradhān and all officers connected with village Kalambe *Tāluka* Parali.

Dated *Suru san saba Shitain mayā va allaf.*

In the place of the *Desmukhi* cess Rupees thirty are annually being paid to *Rājeshri* Joti Anant for feeding Brahmans at the temple of Yavateshwar. This (procedure) is hereby sanctioned. Therefore you should pay it to him from year to year. Last year's balance due should also be paid. Know this. 28th Moon. Order confirmed.

(Seal
Lekhan Sima
the end.)

DOCUMENT No. 16.

Rājārām Narapati
Harsh-nidān
Balājirāv Pradhān.

To

S.R.D.V.R.R. Bālāji Pandit Pradhān and all officers concerned with *Mauje* village Kalambe, Taluka Parali.

Dated *Suma Sitani mayā va allaf.*

The said village has been granted in (*inām*) freehold by *Huzur* to the late *Rājeshri* Joti Anant *Subhedār* of Fort Satara, but last year it was resumed from him and granted to *Rājeshri* Govindrāv Moreshwar as a *Kamāvis* grant for collecting revenue, but the *Huzur* has done the favour as an act of kindness of giving it back to him (*subhedār*) and this *sanad* has been granted. You should therefore co-operate with him, and hand over the village and its revenue to him as before. Govindrāv Moreshwar should be given the work of collecting Government Revenue. 14th *Moharam*. In the presence of *Huzur*

(Seal).

DOCUMENT No. 17.

From

Bālāji Nārāyan Kānhere after compliments.

Appājirāv *Subhedār's* annuity as a *Gadkari* is in vogue as a hereditary grant, and you (the Peshva) have got an order from *Sarkār* to continue such hereditary grants. Therefore in this case the grant should be recovered in the name of *Rājashri* Gangādhar Joti. *Rājashri* Bābāji will apply about this. I enclose a letter to that effect. Therefore the usual grant with the name, assignment, and order by Government under counter-signature should be granted to him. (Submitted) for information.

DOCUMENT No. 18.

Govindrāv Moreshwar
Ever intent upon the
feet of (God) Gajānan.

To

Rājashire Govindrāv Moreshwar Dixit (under Pant Pradhān) and all officers concerned with village Lalhe *tarf* Parali.

Dated *Suma Shitain maya va allaf.*

The said village has been in the possession of *Rājashri* Joti Anant late *Subhedār* of the Fort of Satara, as an *inām* grant from *Huzur*. This year it had been attached by Government, but the attachment has been removed hereby and it has been granted again under former conditions. You should therefore co-operate with him, and pay him the revenue without hitch. Know this. 14th Moon *Mohorum*.

(Seal.)

DOCUMENT No. 19.

Shri Rājārām Narapati
the climax of joy
Mādhavrāv Nārāyan
Mukhya Pradhān.

To

The *Mukhya* Pradhān and all officers concerned with Kalambe, *Tāluka* Parali, *prānt* Wāi.

Dated *Suru san saba sabāin mayā va allaf.*

The *Khālsa* cess, the *Sardeshmukhi* cess, and the proceeds of the Royal garden were resumed from the *Killedār* and granted to *Rājashri* Joti Anant late *subhedār* of Fort Satara. Although from the year of the grants from the Satara budget, they were duly conferred on him, it is reported to *Huzur* that the proceeds thereof are not being paid to him. It is therefore ordered hereby that the proceeds of the said three cesses should be paid to him without hitch. There must be no more complaint about the matter. Know this. 2nd Moon *Rabilākhar*. Order confirmed.

(Seal.)

DOCUMENT No. 20.

It is the wish of the Bombay Government, that the Dewānship of the Baroda state should remain always in the family of Rāvjee Appājee from generation to generation and that his son, brother, nephew, or relatives always be well taken care of by, and receive assistance in every respect, from the Government. Should His Highness the Gāikawar or anybody else raising false calumny against Rāvjee Appājee do him harm while he is conducting his duties with justice, the Company's Government will personally inquire into and decide the matter. Being entrusted with, this day I have signed this paper and sealed it with the seal of the Bombay Government—settled at Khambāyat this 8th day of June 1802.

(Sd.) JONATHAN DUNCAN.

(Seal of the English Government.)

DOCUMENT No. 21.

To

Ajam General Jonathan Duncan, Esquire, President Governor *nisbat* Company Angrez (*sic*)

From

Anandrāv Gāikāvad *Sena Khāskhel, Samsher Bahādur.*

(After compliments.) From the Company Bahādur we received, in our service an army of 2,000 strong with artillery, therefore their salaries shall be paid from the day of the disbandment of our territorial

Shibandi force. The total amount thus payable is Rs. 7,80,000. On this account the villages of *Pargana* Nadiyād yielding annually Rs. 50,000 have been given on lease. The balance of Rs. 7,30,000 shall be paid in cash. On that account the balance available after meeting local expenses from *Pargana* Kaḍi and Bhāvnagar, shall be paid annually. *Rājashri* Bābāji Appāji and Ajam Kamāluddin Husain *Khān Bahādur* stand securities (in this transaction). This agreement shall be fulfilled. Dated 5th Moon *Safar Suma Salās Mayātain va allaf.* What more to write? May our friendship and mutual good will continue.

KAMĀLUDDIN HUSAIN KHĀN BAHĀDUR.

(Seal.) (Seal.)

(Sd.) BĀBĀJI APPĀJI,

(this document is in the handwriting of Rāvji Appāji.)

No. 17.

(the end.)

DOCUMENT No. 22.

To

Shrimant Mahāraj *Swāmi* Chhatrapati,

From

Rāvji Appāji (after obeisance.)

Dated 11th Moon of *Moharam.*

I am as glad as if I have the good fortune of seeing Your Majesty's feet at the receipt of Your Majesty's assuring reply to my letter. At present, agreements have been executed in all provinces of Your Majesty establishing annual payment of revenue. The *mauje* of Kalambe in the district of Parali has been granted to my ancestors by the late Mahārāja. He (my ancestor) was blown up in the bombardment of the fort, after fighting for six months with Emperor Aurangzeb. For that reason the entire village was granted to Prayāgji and we are in the enjoyment thereof (up to date). Recently new taxes were imposed (in the province) but I showed the original documents to *Rājashri* Pant Pradhān and by the grace of Your Majesty set the matter right. Another village *mauje* Navani of the Koregāv *pargana* of the Wāi *Prānt* has been granted to *Rājeshri* Amritrāv Avji Tāmbekar who is employed under our *Sena Khāskhel* (Gāikwād). *Rājashri* Andopant *Kārkun* writes that the orders for the collection of revenue from both the villages will be issued together. I therefore beg to submit this letter (requesting) that such an order should not be passed. They are both (villages) in my possession. If they (orders) have been already issued they may be countermanded as a favour. Your Majesty (will I hope) not mind the fact that I have not been able to render any services direct. No attention be paid to any contrary information placed before (Your Majesty). I wish to pay my respects to your feet. At that time I will render such services as I can. Do not distrust me. How to describe the miseries suffered during forty years after the demise of the late Mahārāja. For twenty-five years I bore all troubles under the Gāikvād. During the last five years Your Majesty's own calf has to feed itself as a suckling of another man's cow. My father has not yet been able to repay the family debts. I have just commenced building a house because even the milkbush (cactus) beams of my cottage have not yet been replaced. An enquiry will reveal the state of the finances here. The state of my household may also be graciously examined. If I am writing falsehood, I swear by Shri Yavateshwar, my family god, and by Your Majesty's feet. In that locality (owing to the trouble the Rāstes have been giving) Kalambe and Palgate have suffered much. Andopant was asked to send my family people to the Konkan but they are mere cripples. They will be better protected near your Highness' (capital) by employing (additional) guards and cavalry. They should not be sent away from the villages. These are rainy days. I have written so. (I beg) Your Majesty (my father and mother) will sanction the necessary arrangement for the protection (of the villages) and will write to me in reply. Thus I submit this letter to Your Majesty.

DOCUMENT No. 23.

Chronicle.

[Compiled by *Vahivātdar* Sadāshiv Nārāyan Abhang dated 6th of the second half of *Mārg Shirsha*, 1803 (*Dhak* era)].

Bhāskar Rāv Vithal says:—

Our ancestor Prayāgji Anant loyally served at Fort Satara in war and peace the late Mahārāja Shrimant

Shāhu Chhatrapati for many years. He faithfully served as Havāldār (commandant) and protected the fort. He had under him all the *Gadkaris* (guards at the fort). His Majesty graciously granted to him by an hereditary grant of one *Kārkun*, one orderly and the villages of Degāv, Jaitājar, Nigdi, Angapur *Taluka* Vadan, Nagawane Shelekvadi, Songav, Dervadital, *Junē*, Gaundi, Kamadi, Raigav, Kudal, and Bambli—together fifteen villages were granted in *sanads* as *ināms*. They are still in the possession of the family. After working at the fort for many years, he was transferred to the Peshvas at Poona. Outside the fort our ancestors and my father, and myself have all along rendered services. We had 500 *gadkaris* under us until 1860-61. Besides these villages, we received dresses of honour. Even after the establishment of the British Government, we were at the head of 500 *gadkaris*. I was at the head, and the Maharāja always respected our position in court. Since 1861-62 (A. D.) the Queen-*sarkār* (direct Rule) discontinued all our active work and granted half the income of the said villages to perpetuity. This grant was made two years ago.

2. During the reign of the late Shāhu Mahārāj Chhatrapati, Emperor Aurangzeb besieged the fort of Satara. At that time our ancestor Prayāgji Anant the chief *subhedār* of the fort, bravely fought at the head of his faithful army. The enemy was defeated and the Mahārāja gained victory. In this battle Prayāgji Anant was blown up during bombardment. He fell towards the Eastern bastion. Mahārāja sent a search party, found him still alive, brought him back, showed him great favour, and finding him loyal and faithful, granted in perpetual *inām* the village of Kalambe. Out of the revenue of his village the *Sardeshmukhi* cess and the

khālsa cess and Royal garden were also granted (after the demise of Prayāgji) to my grand-father Joti Anant, and to Gangādhar Joti and Bhāskar Joti and Rakhmāji Joti, and Sitārām Chimnāji by the late *Shrimant Rājashri* Mādhavrāv Nārāyan Pradhān. We therefore got the entire village. It is in our possession. This *inām* village was granted about 150 years ago. We possess all the documents of the grant.

3. My grand-uncle Rāvji Appāji and grand-father Bābāji Appāji served the Peshva *Sarkār*. Because the were the *subhedārs* of the fort of Satara, they were granted a piece of grass land at *mauje* Akle *tāluka* Satara. We are in the enjoyment of the grant.

4. After the village of Kalambe was granted as *inām* (free-hold), my great grand-uncle Rāvji Appāji and my great grand-father Bābāji Appāji built houses for the *rayyets* and got some of them married at their cost. They supplied food and clothes to the poorest of them. They were religiously disposed and adored God and Brahmans. All the residents of these villages remained contented and happy. I have continued the same policy and have built large houses at Kalambe. They are as follows :—

(1) A mansion in the centre of the town. Built of polished stone, teak blackwood, has four wings, three stories, a first class building, completed in *Shake* 1726 at a cost of three *lākhs* of Rupees. It has no equal (in the district) except in the Palace of Satara.

(2) The temple *Shri* Bhairav, of polished stone, has a high dome and a terrace. Is surrounded by rest-houses and other temples. In its compound there is a temple devoted to Māruti (Hanumān) equally strong and good-looking.

Finished in *Shake* 1730 at a cost of about a *lākh* of rupees (Rs. 1,00,000). I repaired the rest houses in *Shake* 1797 to 1799 at a cost of Rupees 2,000.

(3) In the midst of the town an open-air public masonry seat (*pār*) built of polished stone, in *shake* 1733, cost Rs. 2,000.

(4) The temple of *Shri* Veneshvar on the banks of the Vena river, of polished stone, strong and beautiful. Built in *Shake* 1755, cost Rs. 30,000.

(5) A bathing *ghāt*, of stone and large enough to accommodate 100 people. Cost Rs. 15,000. Has near it two small open-air raised masonry platforms under the adjoining sacred *pipal* (*Ficus religiosa*) tree. Cost Rs. 2,000.

(6) Another separate *ghāt* to the west of the above. Cost Rs. 5,000.

(7) A paved street leading to the river. Cost Rs. 2,000. *Shake* 1734.

5. Our family god *Shri* Yavateshwar has a large temple situated on a hill to the west of Satara. We feel hereditary devotion to that god and have arranged for his worship, his food offerings and for feeding Brahmans, the perpetual light in the temple and annual festivities held on the 30th Moon of *Kārtik* and on the 14th Moon of *Māgh*. The first of these festive occasions has been arranged on a very large scale because our ancestor was in the habit of frequently visiting the hill for paying his respects on this date. Brahmans are fed on that day, *kathās* (dialogue on religious subjects) are held. The annual grant for these two festivities is Rs. 300. This sacred seat of the god is our property. Government have granted a piece of land at Kalambe, yielding Rs. 30 as annual revenue. The difference is paid by me.

6. During my life, I planted an avenue of mango trees along the public road (leading to the hill). This happened eight years ago. These trees are still being nurtured, they have commenced to give shade. I spent up to date about one thousand rupees on (this avenue) and the expenditure will continue.

7. In the Satara District I have village Kalambe as *jahāgir* (free-hold). I have maintained there a Manager (*vabiwātdār*), *kārkuns* (clerks), peons, menial servants, horses, oxen, cows and buffaloes. In cases of disputes, I am represented in the British courts by my managers.

8. On the third Moon of the second half of the month of *Māgh*, a fair is held in the temple of *Shri* Bhairav, god in our village, at our expense and we receive the usual honour.

9. We receive annually our share of the local imports such as 'thatching (*karsai*), merchandise (*kena*), grass, *vāt bigar* (free labour), sugar cane, *til*, and raw sugar (*tilgul*), *etc.*' At present we get through the British Government a modified share of these dues and grant them a receipt.

10. The chief local (dues, due to a *Jahāgirdār*) and to the temple are still paid to us, and the right of igniting the *holi* fire of the village belongs to us. We also receive the first share of the *kadakane* of the *Navarātra* holidays and the *mudis* of *mudi*-full moon.

11. We meet all the expenses of the annual festivities of Yavateshwar.

12. In our manor, there is a temple dedicated to Ganapati (Ganesh). The annual festive ceremonies due in *Bhādrapad* there were held by our ancestors Rāvji Appāji Bābāji Appāji and Vithal Rāo Bābāji on a very grand scale at the expense of Rs. 2,000 a year, but now in

keeping with the times, they are held on a moderate scale.

13. We have three gardens at Kalambe and three well-built wells, an avenue of mango trees, and flower beds.

This is compiled by Mr. Abhang the *Vahilvātdār* of Kalambe and forwarded to Mr. G. R. Gupte, for Dewān Bhāskar Rāv Vithal's approval.

DOCUMENT No. 24.

Shri Mhālsa Kānt.

(Seal.)

From

Anandrāv Gāikwād *Sena Khāskhel Samsher Bahādar,*

To

Bābāji Appāji.

Dated *Suru San Mayātain va allaf.*

You are the hereditary faithful dependant of the *Sarkār,* and now you have successfully carried on the expedition to Karli and have restored order, therefore the *Sarkār* is pleased to appoint you to the *Khāsgi Darak.* You should therefore manage the *Khāsgi Darak* with integrity. Attached is the list of the *Khāsgi* right and cesses. Enjoy these right and cesses (from generation to generation). To ensure its safe enjoyment the English Company *Bahādur* have been offered as a security. Know this. 7th Moon *Ramzan.*

(Seal.)

For maintenance of these rights the English Company *Bahādur* accept the guarantee, *Samvat* 1863.

(*English signature.*)

(Seal).

DOCUMENT No. 25.

Shri Mhālsa Kānt.

(Seal.)

Dated { 1807-8 A. D. / *Samvat* 1864. }

From

Friendly Anandrāv Gāikwād *Sena Khāskhel Samsher Bahādar*,

To

R. R. Bābāji Appāji Khāsgivale.

Dated *Suru San Samān mayātain va allaf.*

The *Sarkār*-state got into heavy debt and was in financial difficulties. You, with the help of the *Ajam* English Company *Bahādur*, settled all account with *Shiledārs*, *Shiband's*, and Artillery, got many sums written off and worked very loyally. In appreciation thereof you are hereby granted the freehold (*inām*) of:—

(1) Village Kamali, (revenue) Rs. 5,000 (a year);

(2) Village Sonevādi *pargana* Ghanadevi (revenue) Rs. 5,000.

Thus two villages yielding Rs. 10,000 a year have been granted by the *Sarkār*. (This grant) includes all rights over water, trees, grass, wood, stone, as well as buried treasure. You can enjoy these villages, from year to year, and from generation to generation. *Sarkār* will continue these grants from generation to generation. Know this. 9th Moon of *Rabilākhar*, duly sealed.

(Seal.)

DOCUMENT No. 26.

Shri Mhālsa Kānt.

(Seal.)

To

All the *Kamāvisdārs*, present and future.

Anandrāv Gāikavād *Sena Khāskhel Samsher Bahādar* (commands) that *Rājashri* Bābāji Appāji Khāsgivale loyally settled the accounts *re* the heavy debt against the *Sarkār* State, with the help of the English *Sarkār* (obtained under instructions). (He) got many sums written off. In appreciation of these services, he has been graciously granted *inām* by the *Sarkār* the villages of Sonevādi (yielding Rs. 5,000) and Berje (yielding Rs. 5,000) from this year. Therefore, transfer to him these villages to perpetuity from generation to generation. It has been entered among the grants (*nemnuk*). No objection need be raised for the annual repetition of this order. Take a copy of this order and return the original to the said (Bābāji Appāji) for enjoyment. Know this. 9th Moon of *Rabilākhar*, duly sealed.

(Seal.)

DOCUMENT No. 27.

Shri Mhālso Kānt.

To

A.Kh. L.A.R.R. Bābāji Appāji,

From

Sena Khāskhel, Samsher Bahādar Anandrāv Gāikavād.

Dated Suru *San Jhide Mayātain va Allaf.*

You have been entrusted with the expedition of *mulukhgiri* in Kathiāwār, Jhalawad, including ours as well as Pant-Pradhān's and Mahikātha-Palanpur tracts. You should therefore settle the sums due, recover them, or arrange through proper securities the recovery thereof from the Mewātis and pay the same into the *Sarkār* Treasury with honesty and integrity. You have been entrusted with this work for three years from the 17th Moon, in the month of *Sābān, Samvat* 1865 to 1867. Therefore perform your duties faithfully (the same day).

(Sealed.)

Registered.

DOCUMENT No. 28.

Memo.

A *Sanad* has been granted to Bābāji Appāji Khāsgivāle on the 17th Moon of *Ramzān*, appointing him

Khāsgi Minister. It contains a list of *Dāilès* (grants): He has to get them in accordance therewith from the beginning of the last year *San Saba Maiyātain*. The following grants are to be hereditary granted on 11th Moon of *Rabilāval* of *Suru San Samari Mayātain va allaf*.

Pargana	Baroda	...	...	Rs.	1,001
,,	Petlavad	...	...	,,	750
,,	Ahmedabad	...	...	,,	750
,,	Vijāpur	...	...	,,	220
,,	Visānagor	...	...	,,	200
,,	Pattan	...	...	,,	700
Zilla	Songad	...	...	,,	200
Pargana	Navasari	...	...	,,	100
,,	Valwād	...	...	,,	100
,,	Tembhe	...	...	,,	200
,,	Kāse Athaval	...	...	,,	100
,,	Mohe	...	...	,,	200
,,	Vadnagar	...	...	,,	200
,,	Molar	...	...	,,	250
,,	Sherior	...	...	,,	300
,,	Kārle	...	..	,,	200
,,	Rājpimple	...	...	,,	300
,,	Modhe	...	...	,,	125
Custom's duty at Savargola in Baroda				,,	250
Kasbe	Umrāt	...	...	,,	30
,,	Jānej	...	...	,,	25
Thāna	Pādre	...	...	,,	125
Pragane	Kherali	...	...	,,	100
Thāna	Chandod	...	...	,,	25
Pragane	Telakwad	...	...	,,	100
,,	Savkhed	...	...	,,	250
,,	Kadi	...	...	,,	575
,,	Kalband	...	...	,,	200
Thāne	Debegav	...	...	,,	100

Pragane Nadiyad	... ...	Rs.	300
" Dhanalke	... ...	"	500
" Kamrej	... ...	"	200
" Varsai	... ...	"	200
" Marali	... ...	"	200
" Kadod	... ...	"	100
" Teladi	... ...	"	350
Duty on the North banks of Tapti	...	"	250
Pragane Vāper	... ...	"	250
" Vaghode	... ...	"	75
" Ghanadevi	... ...	"	250
" Antapur-Vesanpur	...	"	100
" Belsar	... ...	"	350
" Variyav	... ...	"	100
Port Billimor	... ...	"	100
Ramgar Ghāt	... ...	"	50
Pragane Tadkeshwar Poli	...	"	50
" Galhe	... ...	"	200
Mulakhgiri expedition	... ...	"	3,700

Pragane Kathiawar	...	Rs. 2,500
" Mahikallic	...	" 1,200
		Rs. 3,700

Grand Total Rs. 15,001

Total fifteen thousand and one Rupees—Granted from generation to generation from the last year as *Dāyate*, *Mahāl* and *Mulukhgiri*. These grants would therefore recur from year to year and render loyal services. Know this, 11th *Moon Rabilākhar*.

(Granted at) Baroda.

(Sealed.)

DOCUMENT No. 29.

SHRI.

(Mhālsa Kānt)

MEMORANDUM.

Rājashri Bābāji Appāji Khāsgivāle has been entrusted since the last year with the duties of the hereditary office and a *Sanad* has been granted on the 17th Moon of the month of *Ramzān*. A separate list of the grants (in connection therewith) has been given therein. In accordance therewith the following grants about the *Shiledārs* and *Pāgedārs* and *Shibandi* have been made from the beginning of the last year *San Sabba Mayātain*. (Dated 11th Moon of *Rabilākhar Suru San Mayātain va allaf.*)

(1) For each Siledār, Rupee one per year has been promised. It may be received (by him).

(1) The *Huzrāt Pāga* and *Pathaki Pāga* ½ Rupee per each cavalry man (*sawār*).

(1) The grants recorded by the "Master of the Seal" (Shikenavis may also be paid).

In connection with the hereditary office, these are the grants sanctioned for *Shiledār*, *Pāga* and *Shibandi* ; they may be paid. He may receive them and render loyal and faithful services to the *Sarkār*. Know this 11th Moon *Rabilākhar*. Camp Baroda.

Registered.

(Sealed).

DOCUMENT No. 30.

To

Ajam, Bābāji Sāheb Jādā Hu,

From

Ajdil, *Aikhalās*, Major Walker Sāheb, *Salām bājad Salām.*

After knowing the good news of this place (be so good as to) inform how do you do?

Further, Ajam Rangrām Bhavāni Joshi (?) has been appointed as a representative (*abdār*). This (letter) has been written to inform you of the fact. Whenever therefore you will go to that (?) province, protect his forts and villages. You will not try to exact your usual dues on them. Do not take notice of what untoward things his enemies may tell you. His manager Ajam Bhavānji Rāmji Meheta will see you. He should be welcomed and treated well. Despatched on 31st *Saffar* 12th June, 1823. What more to write? Be kind and friendly.

(*English signature.*)

DOCUMENT No. 31.

Samvat 1863.

Issued on the 13th Moon of *Rajab*, Thursday *San Sabā Maiyātain*, *Bhāndrapad* 4th of the first half (*shuddh*). Camp Kudal near fort Kadi.

To

Ajam Bābāji Sāheb Jādā Mohabat Hu.

A friendly communication.

After compliments,—

Major Walker presents *salām Bājat salām.* After hearing news from here, (please) keep informed of your welfare.

Your letter No. 4 of *Rajab* to *Ajam* Bāpu Mairāl has been received and contents (thereof) have been known as interpreted by Gangādhar Shāstri. You have shown many despondent thoughts. They all seem to deserve consideration. But the plan I have formed is unshakable. Bāpu will tell you all its details. You will know. You should therefore entertain no doubt about it. I shall give you copies of the former and present state agreements. Do not delay your arrival. Dated 23rd September, 9th Moon 1806 A. D. What more to write? Entertain friendly feelings is the request (of)

(*English signature*).

DOCUMENT No. 32.

To

Ajam Bābāji Sāheb Camp Lashkar
(*Jādā Mohabat.*)
(*Saheb Mshfala Meherban Lasu Farman Dost.*)

From

Meherbān Major Walker.

After compliments,—

You may have learnt all details after the visit of Bāpu Mairāl. Come soon in accordance therewith. Bāpu Mairāl wrote a letter to Gangādhar Shāstri. In it, he said that the *Gārdis* should be deputed to confront the *Moghias*. You need not be anxious about it in the least. Bābāji Sāheb, there is no difference between your life and honour, and my life and honour (they are, identical).

Be quite sure of this and come with full confidence. It will be well if you live here after the visit, if not, after obtaining the permit from *Azam* Mahārāja Anandrāv Gāikavād *Senākhāskhel Samsher Bahādar*, you will be allowed to go with honour. Come to your work. To assure you, a letter from the Governor General has been despatched yesterday and to-day this letter is being written. I and my Government are always ready to support all the people of the late Rāvba Saheb. Among these you are equal to him in rank and are his brother. Therefore entertain no suspicion. You will on careful consideration realize the motive of my hard work.

Bābāji Sāheb! this private letter is being addressed to you as an assurance. *Azam* Sitārām Rāvji has already written to you. Write to him in reply that you are coming forthwith because *he* has written to you, but that you have written to Major *Sāheb* for a letter from the *Shrimant*. Then write a letter to me that your nephew has written to you an urgent letter and therefore (I) should send you a Government letter and a letter from the Mahārāja. Write (to me) like this. I shall then send a letter from my Government to the Mahārāja. But do not delay. Come.

Dated 25th August, 10th Moon *Jamādilākhar* 1806 A.D. What more to write? Keep kind is the request of

MAJOR WALKER.

DOCUMENT No. 33.

To

Ajam Bābāji Sāheb *Jāda Mohabat Hu.*

(After compliments.) After I left Baroda I received some letters from the Government of Bombay regarding some communications from the Governor-General about Baroda. In all these papers both the Governments mention your excellent work in faithfully serving the Gāikwād *Sarkār* and administering his state. On the successful termination of this arrangement, it will ensure the success of the proposal of your Chief, and Government will help you in the accomplishment of your wishes expressed.

Secondly, the Governor has sent a letter to Sitārām Bāpu with Bandhuji, containing reference to your work. I would have written to you about it even if I were there, but as I am not present there I give only a short purport.

Bābāji Sāheb! on hearing that a letter came direct with Bandhuji, there should be no other thought. The letter contains general approval of your work. You should therefore continue your work and bring it to conclusion. The Governor thinks that the duty you have been performing for your Chief so cleverly and laboriously, should be an accomplished fact and that he should write to you a complimentary letter about the successful achievement of the scheme. Be assured therefore that the Government does reserve its opinion and does not express it. Not that they do not know it. Government know for certain, that on the attainment of the success of the *Sarkār's* scheme, the Gāikwād will love you better. That will happen and the Company's Government afford their protection to you and yours, as regards their happiness. Be informed. Dated 8th September, 1807 A. D. 5th Moon *Rajjab*. What more to write?

(*Signature of Major Walker.*)

DOCUMENT No. 34.

(Seal.)

To

Ajam Major Walker Sāheb, etc., etc.,

From

Anandrāv Gaikwād *Sena Khāskhel Samsher Bahādar.*

(After compliments.) *Rājeshri* Bābāji Appāji has been performing his duties to the state in an excellent manner. Now he has successfully carried out the *Mulukhgiri* Expedition of Kathiawar. On his return, he has been entrusted with the hereditary duties of the *Khāsgi Darak*. *Chiranjiv* Sitārām Rāvji has been instructed to issue the requisite *sanads*. I hope therefore that you will co-operate and ensure the guarantee of the Company Government to its perpetual continuity. Let the *sanads* be prepared as early as possible I must give him the dress of honour.

Suru San Saba Mayātain va allaf.

(*Signature of Anandrāv Gaikavād.*)

Do in accordance with this writing 12th Moon *Sābān*.

Registered.

(Seal.)

DOCUMENT No. 35.

A.D. 1807
Samvat 1863

Shri Mhālsa Kānt
(Seal.)

To

A. L. A. R. R. Bābāji Appāji,

From

Anandrāv Gaikwād *Sena Khāskhel Samsher Bahādar.*
Dated *Suru San Saba Mayātain va allaf.*

You have all along been rendering honest and loyal services to the *Sarkār*. Now the diplomatic work about Kadi and the expedition to Kathiawar have been creditably accomplished. The work of the *Khāsgi Darak* has therefore been entrusted to you. Do therefore faithfully carry on the duties of the *Darak* and enjoy hereditarily the grants made in connection therewith. The *Ajam* English Company stand as a friendly guarantee. Know this 7th *Moon Ramzān.*

(Sealed.)

In accordance herewith the English Company *Bahādur*—stand in friendly guarantee.

(*English signature.*)

(English Seal.)

DOCUMENT No. 36.

To

Ajam Bābāji Sāheb *Jamedār Mahatāb Hu,*

From

Col. Alexander Walker, Resident.

(After compliments.) I am in haste to go to my country. Therefore before leaving this place I wish to write to you more or less.

You have rendered valuable services to the Gaikwād state. A letter has therefore been sent to *Ajam* Fattesing Rāo Sāheb. In it the description of your loyal services has not been omitted because (it is desired) that he should always be kind to you. Be assured of this. On my going to Bombay, the Governor in Council will be informed of your loyal services, and that will lead to your prospects for ever.

I remember that your great achievements at Baroda proved less expensive than the amount you received from the State Treasury. That led to the reduction of the state debt.

Therefore Bābāji Sāheb ! It is not necessary to describe these matters to you. You know them all. But the reason of recording them here is to draw your attention to the perpetuation of the most important achievements. You are aware of this fact also. It is an arrangement to the advantage of the Gaikwād and Government have the credit. They are therefore sure that the work will be continued under your mature guidance. It is not necessary to add more about your mature experience. I am sorry I have to part with you as a friend. May you fare well. May you be happy and always write to me. Dated 21st Moon *Jilkād* 10th January 1809. What more to write?

(*English signature.*)

26th *Jilkād*
Paushya Vadya 12th
San tisā Mayātain va allaf
1865.

DOCUMENT No. 37.

27th Moon *Rabilāval*
Āshādh month
San 1858.

Article 10 of the 3rd Treaty.

ARTICLE 10. We agree to the articles discussed with Major Walker, to my state and lineal successors and *Dewān* Rāvji Appāji and his sons, brothers, relations, friends and Mādhavrāo Gopāl Mazumdār may be helped by the Company Bahādur and none may be allowed to combine against another. On this Major Walker admits that your (Gāikwād's) state will remain under the regime of your family and that the Minister's (*Divāngi·i*) post shall continue from generation to generation unto the family of the said (Rāvji Appāji). The Company stand as a security and your (Gāikwād's) *vakil* will discuss (matters) in the presence of our (the British) *vakil*.

DOCUMENT No. 38.

To

Ajam Akram Mahārāj Anandrāo Gaikavād *Sena Khāskhel, Samsher Bahādār Jāda Ekbāl Hu,*

From

Col. Alexander Walker, Resident.

(After compliments.) Received Mahārāja's letter dated 29th Moon *Ramjan.* Considering the faithfulness of *Ajam* Gangādhar Shāstri the trusted *Māmledār* of the Honourable Company's Government. Mahārāja, (it says), intends granting him a village in free-hold and asks permission to do so. We approve of the step in appreciation of his loyalty. He deserves it. The Company's Government feel sure of it. The permission will therefore not be refused. I therefore have the pleasure to write that in order to attain success in this work, I have granted him leave to go. 26th Moon *Savāl,* dated 15th December 1808. What more to write? Keep friendly.

(*English signature.*)

Tisa Sabain
Mayātain va allaf
San 1865.

DOCUMENT No. 39.

To

Ajam *Akram* Mahārāj Anandrāo Gāikavād *Sena Khāskhel Shamsher Bahādar Jādā Ekbāl Hu*,

From

Col. Alexander Walker, Resident.

(After compliments.) Since I left you (I remember) our conversation in which you spoke about yourself and the Company's Government and that on being informed the Company should assist you in just ways. I have therefore written to Fattesing Rāv Bābāsāheb Gāikavād and to *Ajam* Bābāji Appāji Khāsgivāle giving my final opinion. You too will (it is hoped) act in consultation with them both and do credit to the State. I shall be glad to hear in England of the increasing friendship between you and the Company's Government. 24th Moon *Jilkād*, dated 21st January, 1809. What more to write? Be friendly.

26th Moon *Jilkād*, *Paushya Vadya* 12th
San Tisa Maytain va allaf 1865.

(*English signature.*)

DOCUMENT No. 40.

(Seal.)

To

Ajam General Jonathan Duncan, Esqr., (*sic*)
President & Governor, Company *Ingraj Bahādar Jāda Mohabat Hu*,

From

Anandrāv Gāikavād *Sena Khāskhel Samsher Bahādar*.

(After compliments.) Company *Ingraj* Bahādur placed at the disposal of my State 2,000 soldiers besides artillery. The pay of this force will commence on the day of the disbandment of our *sibandi* force. It is therefore not possible to pay the expenses of the first year. Therefore the total amount payable is Rs. 7,80,000 (Seven *lakhs* and eighty thousand) for twelve months. In part payment of this sum, villages yielding Rs. 50,000. a year from *Pargane* Nadiad have been handed over. The balance of Rs. 7,30,000 (Seven *lakhs* and thirty thousand Rupees) shall be paid in cash. Deducting the expenses, the savings out of the fort and *mahāl* of Kadi and the Bhavnagar boundary, and balance out of the year 1857-58 from Kathiawar and from other items, we shall repay these seven *lakhs* and thirty thousand with interest at the rate of As. 12 per cent. We shall pay. For securities we offer *Bahādur Rājeshri* Bābāji Appāji and *Ajam* Kamaluddin Husen *Khān Bahādur*. Payments will be made in accordance herewith. 5th Moon *Suru San Salās Matyāain va allaf.* What more to write? Be kind and friendly.

(Seal.)

Bābāji Appāji
Dastūr Rāoji Appāji)
Kamāluddin Husen Khān Bahādur.

DOCUMENT No. 41.

MEMO of questions raised by Ajam Fattesing Rão Gaikavād *Suru ashar Mayātain va allaf.*

Q. I. The *Modikhāna* is closed. It should always be kept working.

Reply. Rs. 3,00,000 (three *lākhs*) have been assigned for the *Modikhāna* and Rs. 36,000 (thirty-six thousand) for *Annachchatra* (free food). Thus three *lākhs* and thirty-six thousand Rupees may be expended every year. If this sum is not exceeded it will remain working for ever.

Q. I. The cavalry men are inconvenienced for want of payment.

Reply. There would have been no inconvenience, if the *pāga* (cavalry) could have been managed in accordance with the provision in the budget. Expenditure has increased and no provision has been made for the outlay. I wish to examine the accounts of the state and to regulate the outlay. Instead of that the expected increase of revenue in some *Mahāls*, will be absorbed by increased expenditure. It will result in loss to the *Sarkār* and anxiety to me. I am in this doubt. But if the outlay is regulated in accordance with the budget, some arrangement will be made to meet the extra expenditure incurred at your pleasure.

Q. I. There is trouble in some *Mahāls.*

Reply. The Pattan and Ahmedabad *Mahāls* have not kept their promises and created confusion. Bābāji has promised to adjust matters about Ahmedabad. If Pattan-matters be settled likewise, all troubles will soon cease.

"I agree to your proposals." Hearing these words of acceptance, I am sending this memorandum, which may be followed in practice.

"RECORD OF NOTES TAKEN" *San* 1866.

DOCUMENT No. 42.

San 1866.

To

Rāosāheb Mushfala Kadardān Lark Gustar Mukhlisanal Anandrāv Gāikvād *Sena Khākhel Samsher Bahādar.*

From

The Honourable Korva (?)
Elphinstone Sāheb Bahādur.

(After compliments.) Received letter from *Meherbān* (you) dated 2nd Moon *Safar* sent through Bāpu Mairā and contents known. There will be no neglect on your friend's (my) part in doing the work of the *Darbār.* Know this. 16th Moon April. What more to write? Be kind and friendly.

(*English signature.*)

DOCUMENT No. 43.

Notes.

Vithalrāv Bābāji: Bābāji Sāheb died in *Samvat* 1867. At that time he, (Vithalrāv,) returned from Amedabad in the month of *Kārtik* and administered the state conjointly with Gangādhar Shāstri, Vakil of the Company's Government under Fattesing Rāv, who was a *Mutālik* (Deputy). Then Fattesing Rāv and Gangādhar Shāstri went to Kathiāwār for the Nagar-expedition. After return, Gangādhar Shāstri obtained the *Khillāt* from the Gāikvād, and went to Poona as a *Vakil.* He engaged the services of Bābā Marāthe and Yeshvant Dāda Godbole. They, and Vithalrāv Bābāji conjointly carried on the duties of the state. Then Yeshvantrāv Dāda was dismissed, and Gangādhar Shāstri died. Then with the consent of the Resident Colonel Sāheb, Vithalrāv Bābāji carried on the duties. The Company Government decided that there should be another officer, and the Colonel Sāheb brought Dhākji Dādāji from Bombay and employed him. Dhākji Dādāji took Umiāshankar under him and worked with Vithalrāv Bābāji under Fattesingrāv Bābāsāheb in his palace. Then Fattesingrāv Bābāsāheb died and Anandrāv Mahārāja appointed Sayājirāv as his *Mutālik* (Deputy). At that time Vithalrāv Bābāji and Dhākji Dādāji attended office in the place of Sayājirāv Mahārāj. Then after the demise of Anandrāv Gāikvād, Sayājirāv Mahārāj became the Gāikavād. At that time these two officers were the ministers. Then Elphinstone Sāheb came to Baroda, and adjusted the administration of the state and appointed Vithalrāv Bābāji and Sayājirāv as his chief helpers. After this, the officers of the Company were all dismissed. Sayāji Mahārāja, however, retained the services of Vithalrāv Devāji for his *Khāsgi* Department.

After he began his work, some defalcations were discovered against Umiāshankar. He was dismissed. Dhākji Dādāji was also dismissed. Then Vithalrāv Bābāji and Vithalrāv Devāji worked together (as ministers). But the *Sarkār* relied on Vithalrāv Devāji. However, Vithalrāv Devāji commanded the respect of the *Sarkār* and continued to work.

Then on account of the diplomacy of the '7th year,' *Sarkār* lost confidence in Vithalrāv Devāji and he was dismissed, and Venirām Aditrām was deputed from Bombay to Calcutta. At this time, Vithalrāv Bābāji and Bhāu Purānik were carrying on the duties (of the minister). Then Vithalrāv Bābāji was taken ill and lost consciousness, and Krishnarāv Bhagwant was asked to work in the *Khāsgi* Department. Krishnarāv and Bhāu Purānik worked together. Then Vithalrāv Devāji mortgaged seven *Mahāls* of the state to pay off its debt. At this time Vithalrāv Bābāji died, and Bhāskarrāv Vithal was adopted. Vithalrāv Devaji went to Dabhai and thence to Kadi to administer the seven *Mahāls*. The administration of the state was entrusted to Bhāu Purānik and Krishnarāv Bhagwant on behalf of Bhāskarrāv Vithal. Bhāskarrāv was at that time 12 years of age, and therefore these two officers were appointed by the *Sarkār* and Gopāl Pant was working in the *Khāsgi* Department on behalf of Venirām. But while in state-affairs Krishnarāv Bhagwant and Bhāu Purānik were working, the *Sarkār* appointed Gopāl Pant as *Sikenevis*. The seven *Mahāls* were at this time released. He began working with the attachments of properties in connection therewith. Our agents Krishnarāv Bhagwant and Gopāl Pant fell out, and Krishnarāv was dismissed. Then Venirām Aditrām returned to Bombay from Calcutta. When he came to Baroda from there, Gopāl Pant was dismissed and Venirām Aditrām assumed the title of *Himmat Bahādur*, and worked (as Minister). He asked Bhāskarrāv to pay him one per cent. as Vakil's *Dasturi*. Bhāskarrāv refused. Venirām therefore became his enemy and stopped him from attending even the *Darbār*. Since then there is no one to work on behalf of Bhāskarrāv and he does not attend. After some years he began attending the Darbār. (This is already known.)

Shrāvan Vadya 2nd Tuesday *Samvat* 1910 *Shak* 1776.

DOCUMENT No. 44.

Camp, Kudal near Fort Kadi.

13th Moon *Rajjab*, *Bhādrapad*
sudh 14th (Thursday)
San *Sabā Mayātain*.

To

R. R. R. Bābāji Sāheb,

From

Gangādhar Shāstri Patvardhan.

(After blessings.) I am quite well at Baroda up to the 9th Moon of *Rajjab*. I saw the letters you sent to *Rajeshri* Bāpu on the 4th Moon, and learnt their contents. You wrote to Bāpu in a despondent tone and prevented him from going to Kadi and asked him to live in Bombay after rendering accounts. I learn all this. Bābāsāheb! when you come to Dakore I and the Colonel Sāheb will both see you. You and he will learn all details. Had I taken this step I should have been guilty of ruining your family. I cannot give details here. Bāpu will explain (details). I also will explain. Then you will realize the whole affair. As you have placed your head on my thigh, come at once. If on your arrival any changes be affected in the former arrangements, no one will blame (you). But that will be the climax of confidence, and you will realize that in this mortal world people are born of one set of parents only. I have asked Bāpu to go ahead to bring you. Do not be angry with him. Let me know the day of your arrival at Dākore. The Colonel Sāheb is coming and arrangement must be made for his guards, baggage, etc. I am also very sorry to see that letter, so was the Colonel Sāheb. You will know all from the letter addressed to you. That letter has been forwarded to the officer of our Government who lives at Kadi. It has been sent through that place to ensure confidential despatch.

Bābāsāheb! if in accordance with the writing (I) have to go to Bombay, Benares is also in the possession of the Company, and it is nearer. As you are the senior and have the authority of a *guru* (teacher) and as I and Bāpu are your pupils, we shall live by begging. We swear that we have no other wish. Be assured. Let Bāpu have audience as soon as possible. That will remove all misunderstanding from your mind.

Bhādrapad suddh 11th Tuesday, at 2 *ghatikās*. May you be informed. This letter has been included in the English letters and has therefore not been sealed. The seal will increase the size of the envelope. Compliments.

DOCUMENT No. 45.

To

Elphinstone Major (*sic*) Walker Sāheb, Baroda.

Under instructions from the General Sāheb of Bombay, Grant Sāheb wrote that Rāvji Appāji the influential intelligent Minister of the Gāikavād State died, therefore you should inform *Shrimant Rājeshri* Anandrāv Gāikavād *Sena Khāskhel Samsher Bahādur*, and *Shri* Sitārām Rāvji the adopted son of the deceased, and Bābaji Appāji his brother ; and all the (first class) members of the family that the Government of Bombay and its Ministers are very sorry. The assistance rendered by the Company Government to the deceased, his position, and to his relations shall be continued on similar lines. During the career of the deceased *Divān*, the State of Baroda was protected owing to the friendship (alliance) he formed between them. You all remained true to your salt, and trustingly administered the State and the Gujerat *Prānt* They may be assured that the State and the *Rayots* of Gujerat will continue to be kept safe.

(Dated) *Shrāvan Shuddh* 7th.

DOCUMENT No. 46.

Shri Mhālsa Kānt.

Memo. of grants conferred in appreciation of the services of the late Rāvji Appāji the father of *Rājeshri* Sitarām Rāvji, under the late Govindrāv Maharāja. In order to make suitable provision the *Sarkār* has graciously been pleased (to sanction) these grants on *Suru San Sabain Ashar Maiyàtain va allaf*:—

Amount Rupees:—

23,000 *Mauje* Sadhali *Pragane* Senor and *Mauje* Botane *Pragane* Ahmedabad—the total Revenue of both the villages.

6,000 for *Sāliāna* to Huzur equipage.

11,000 Cash to be paid through the *Potdār* every year.

The Garden. In *Mavje* Mate *Pragane* Chanraish and the grant from the English *Bahādur*—Rs. 20,000.

In this manner the annual grant amounting to Rs. 40,000 (forty thousand) and Rs. 20,000 (twenty thousand) from the *Ajam* Company's *Sarkār*, total sixty thousand Rupees to be paid from *san tisa Mayātain, Samvat* 1868. Some creditors have been sitting in *dharna* at his door. To conciliate them Rs. 1,10,000 (one *lākh* and ten thousand) have been advanced through Pārakhs Samal Buhar and Mangal Sukhidās and Hari Bhakti and Mairāl Nārāyan and Kushāl Chand Ambaidās] Pārakh. For writing off old debts Rs. 30,000 (thirty thousand) have been assigned out of these grants. The balance of Rupees left is thirty thousand. He (Sitāram) should live happily with this income. Know this 9th Moon *Ramzān*. Camp Baroda (sealed). A sealed copy has been carried to the Bungalow by Bābàji Vithal of the Muzumdar's establishment on the same day.

DOCUMENT No. 47.

Shri Mhālsa Kānt.

(SEAL.)

To

Chiranjiv Rājeshri Sitārām Rāvji,

From

Anandrāv Gāikavād *Sena Khāskhel Samsher Bahādur.*

(After blessings.) Your late father Rāvji Appāji's Divānship has been conferred on you. Do perform (the duties) in the manner your father did by ensuring friendship with the English Bahādur, and in such a way as to increase that relation and to prevent all disturbances in my state as you have been doing heretofore, and arrange for the perpetuity of my state, demolish all enemies of the state by ensuring the perpetual observance of the mutual agreements between this state and the English Bahādur. Nobody should be allowed to override the other. In case any of my descendants will not behave well and will do harm to the state or disturb our friendly relation and will behave unjustly, if you and the English Bahādur are satisfied, you can select from my descendants one who is just and fit to rule, and brave, and instal him and carry on the duties and protect the state. The sacred promises between the late Govindrāv Mahārāj and you as regards the perpetuity of our Rāj and your Divānship shall be observed for ever. My descendants shall not interfere with you and your descendant's rights, and therefore the administration and authority of the state is entrusted to you. Therefore maintain friendly relation with the English Bahādur and protect the state and protect the *ryots* of this territory. All these affairs are entrusted to you. Your descendants and my descendants should trust one another. 17th Moon *Rabilākhar, Suru San arba Maiyātain va allaf.* What more to write? Blessings.

(Seal.)

DOCUMENT No. 48.

Shri Mhālsa Kānt.

(SEAL.)

To

Chiranjiv Rājeshri Bhāskarrāv Vithal Khāsgivāle,

From

Sayājirāv Gāikavād *Sena Khāskhel, Samsher Bahādur*..

Dated *Suru San Tisa Asharin Maiyātain va allaf.*

(After blessings.) Your father Vithalrāv Bābāji Khāsgivāle was taken ill and was on the point of death. At that time under instructions from the *Sarkār* he religiously adopted you as his son. Then he expired, and therefore this *Sanad* is being granted to you. In accordance with document dated 7th Moon *Jiikād* containing seven items, your father Vithalrāv Bābāji received a *sanad* in *Ihide ashar Maiyātain* with the guarantee of the Company Bahādur. In the same manner you are appointed (hereby) to carryon the duties of the Khāsgi *Darak*. You should therefore manage the Khāsgi *Darak* as stated in the memoranda separately granted. Those grants will be continued to you. You should enjoy them from generation to generation and serve the *Sarkār* honestly and loyally. No untoward thing will take place regarding you and your relations. The Company Bahādur stand guarantee in the just way. Know this. 6th Moon *Safar*. Blessings.

[Copy.]

(Seal.) (English Seal.)

(*English signature.*)

DOCUMENT No. 49.

Notes.

1. Rāvji Appāji came from Poona in *Samvat* 1850. He worked (as minister) for 9 years.
1. Sitārām Rāvji and Sakhārām Chimnāji worked (as *Kārbhāri*) up to 1862 for about 3 years.
1. Bābāji Appāji worked (as minister) from *Samvat* 1863 to the month of *Kārtik Samvat* 1867.
1. Vithalrāv Bābāji and Gangādhar Shāstri (as long as he was at Baroda) worked amicably together. When Gangādhar Shāstri went to Poona in *Samvat* 1870, the duties were carried on in consultation with Bābā Marāthe and Yashvantrāv Dāda Godbole. After Gangādhar Shāstri's death, Yashvantrāv Godbole was under the displeasure of the *Sarkār* and he was dismissed. Bābā Marāthe was working. Then Ajam Colonel Sāheb Bahādur brought Dhākji Dādāji from Bombay. Vithalrāv Bābāji was working through him. After the demise of Anandrāv Mahārāja, Mahārāja Sayājirāv succeeded him to the *gādi*, then Vithalrāv Bābāji and Dhākji Dādāji were working together. Umia Shankar was under them. Dhākji Dādāji went to Bombay, and Umia Shankar was dismissed. It was then decided that Vithalrāv Dewāji be brought from Kathiawar. He (Vithalrāv Bābāji) worked until then.
1. Vithal Dewāji the *Karkun* of the Khāsgivale's family was employed to do the work (of the minister). He worked in co-operation with Vithalrāv Bābāji until *Samvat* 1883. He (Vithalrāv Devāji) then went to Kabani Mahāl.
1. In *Samvat* 1884 Vithalrāv Bābāji was taken ill, and therefore while Krishnarāv Bhagwant and Bhāu

Purānik were conjointly carrying on his duties Vithalrāv Bābaji died. Bhaskarrāv Vithal was a minor, and therefore Krishnarāv Bhagwant carried on the duties until *Samvat* 1885.

1. In *Samvat* 1886, Venirām Aditrām kept Gopāl Pānt at Baroda and went to Bombay. Gopālrāv carried on the duties until the end of *Samvat* 1888.

1. In 1889, Venirām Aditrām returned from Bombay, removed Gopāl Pant, and worked until 1893. He was hostile to the *Bahādarivāllās* (guarantee holders). He ran away to Calcutta. At this time Ganesh Pant Bhāu Oze, a subordinate of the Phadnis family, worked (as minister) until the death of Sayāji Rāv Mahārāja and thereafter Raghunāthrāv Dhāyabar, Govindrāv Pandurāng Rode and Ganesh Bhāu Oze carried on the duties, until the end of *Samvat* 1905.

1. Since the *Ashādh* of *Samvat* 1906, Govindrāv Pandurāng Rode, Raghunāthrāv Dhāyabar, and Vithal Khanderāv Tāmbekar were carrying on the duties (of the minister). In *Samvat* 1907, the others did the same without consulting Raghunāthrāv Dhāyabar. When Govindrāv Rode returned from Bombay he resigned (or was dismissed) and Vithal Khanderāv Tāmbekar carried on the duties.

DOCUMENT No. 50.

Chronicle.

Notes.—Govindrāv Gāikavād got the *khillāt* of *Sena Khāskhel* on *Bhādrapad Shudh* 7th.

1. Govindrāv Gāikavād *Sena Khāskhel Samsher Bahādur* died on the 2nd Moon of the first half of *Ashvin, Samvat* 1856-1857.

1. The senior Fattesing Gāikavād *Sena Khāskhel Samsher Bahādur* received the dress of honour of "*Sena Khāskhel Samsher Bahādur.*" He died in *Shak* 1712 *Samvat* 1847.

1. When Fattesing Gāikawād died, after he was cremated, Mānāji Gāikavād took charge of Baroda after Yādav Bhāskar. He declared himself the *Sardār*, but received no dress; died in *Samvat* 1856.

1. Fattesing Gāikavād, *Kārbhāri Mutālik, Samsher Bahādur, Samvat* 1874-1877. Died on the 6th Moon of the bright half of *Jeshth.*

1. Ānandrāv Gāikavād *Sena Khāskhel Samsher Bahādur*, (from) *Jeshtha Samvat* 1874 to 1876. On the 15th Moon of the first half of *Ashvin*, 1876 he died at Bhāvnagar.

1. On the 7th Moon of the dark half of *Mārgashirsha, Sena Khāskhel Samsher Bahādur* Sayājirāv Gāikavād died.

1. On Tuesday the 7th Moon of the dark half of *Kārtik*, Ganpatrāv Gāikavād *Sena Khāskhel Samsher Bahādur* died.

1. On Monday the 6th Moon of the bright half of *Mārgashirsha* Khanderāv Mahārāj died at Makarpura.

DOCUMENT No. 51.

Chronicle.

Notes on old history :—

1. In *Samvat* 1249 *Shak* 1714 Govindrāv Mahārāj was installed. He came to Gujerat in *Samvat* 1850.

2. In *Samvat* 1851 Rāvba Bāba met (him) at Nāsik and came to Gujerat.

3. In *Samvat* 1853 Bābāji Appāji got the dress (appointment) of Mahikātha.

4. In *Samvat* 1855 he got the dress (appointment) of Ahmedabad.

5. In *Samvat* 1856 Malhār Rāv carried on the expedition.

6. In *Samvat* 1856 assistance of the English was obtained and Rāvba Bāba received the *Bahādari.*

7. In *Samvat* 1858 Rāvba Bāba died.

8. In *Samvat* 1863 Bābāji Appāji got the appointment of the Khāsgi *Darak.* Received *Bahādari*; he got four appointments created synchronously.

9. In the *Kārtik* of *Samvat* 1865 Bābāji Appāji died.

10. In *Samvat* 1866 Bāpu Mairāl was sent to Poona as a *vakil,* then it was recorded that Rāvji Malhār had no share in it (the appointment).

11. In *Samvat* 1874 Bājirav Peshvā ran away and the English became the masters.

12. In *Samvat* 1867 Fattesingrāv Gāikavād died.

13. In *Samvat* 1878 Dādāsāheb Gāikavad died and Sayāji Mahārāja succeeded him. The following are the names of the Kārbhāris of his regime :

1. Vithalrāv Bābāji Khāsgivāle.
1. Vithalrāv Devāji Devānji.
1. Bhāu Purānik (Kushāba Māma).

1. Gopāl Krishna Devdhar.
1. Venirām Bhāi.
1. Gopālrāv Mairāl.
1. Ganesh Pant Bhāu of the Fadnis' establishment.

14. In *Samvat* 1904 Sayājirāv Mahārāja died and Ganapadrāv Mahārāja succeeded him. His Kārbhāris were:

1. Ganesh Pant Bhāu.
1. Bhāu Tāmbekar.
2. ....

15. In *Samvat* 1904 Ganpatrāv Mahārāja received the reins. He died in *Samvat* 1913 and was succeeded by Khanderāv Mahārāja.

16. On the 6th Moon of the bright half of *Margashirsha* of 1927 Khanderāv Mahārāja died.

DOCUMENT No. 52.

Chronicle.

SUMMARY of historical notes on the conquest of Gujerat by *Sena Khāskhel Samsher Bahādur* the Gāikavād of Baroda collected by Raghunāth Laxman Chitnis at the request of Gangādhar Shastri who wanted them for submission to the Peshva *Sarkār* and to the Company *Sarkār*.

Pilājirāv Gāikavād was the *Patel* of Bhor. He was pressed hard for some debt due to the *Sarkār*. He migrated to the banks of the Godāvari and Bhima. One night, he reached the house of his sister. A *Subha* of the Bijapur state reached the same village the next day on his way from Delhi. His army was marching at midday, and rested under the trees. Among the retinue there were horses, caparisoned with gold and silver ornaments, and covered with gold embroidered cloths. Some were sleeping and some went to buy stimulants, tobaccos, pipes, etc. Pilāji selected a fine horse. Its *syce* was snoring. The others left the place. When Pilāji saw that the *syce* near whom he was sitting was fast asleep, he mounted the horse and started with the army. When he reached an adjoining river, he halted with the excuse of allowing the horse to drink water and then began to go away in a different direction. Some one saw, and threatened him. Pilāji gave a blow and the man fell wounded from his horse. He continued his career through the mountainous country. On the third or fourth day he reached Visarvāda where the Bānde *Sardār* had a large stable for stallions. One of Pilāji's relations was employed there as the keeper of the grains. He fed the horse, got it groomed, and found accommodation for it. Pilāji related his short adventure to the grain keeper. Both of them decided to go to Sangad the following day. *Sardār* Bānde was there with his army. Finding Pilāji an active and clever man, he was employed (with his new horse) at Rs. 2 per day. He quickly rose by good hard work carrying messages, settling disputes, and arresting runaways.

Pilājirāv's eldest son was Sayājirāv, second Anandrāv and the third Malharrāv. He had four more sons besides 16 born of remarriages. He added five to twenty-five horses of his own and engaged a hundred or two belonging to *Shiledārs*. Deciding the boundary cases in Maval, arranging mutual settlements in local disputes, and collecting a few rupees from every "customer," was his good luck. Those who attacked him were defeated in pitched battles. Their heads were severed. He therefore achieved success in all directions. He wished to invade Surat. He went to Surat. He looted the town, captured the *sāwkārs*. In negotiating their release the *Sarkār* accepted Pilāji's guarantee for *lākhs* of rupees and people willingly trusted him.

When the Peshva came (to that place ?) the Dābhāde proposed that he should not be allowed to do so. He advanced to Dabhai and fought a battle with Dādāsāheb (Raghunāthrāv Peshva). Dābhāde was killed on the battle-field. Pilāji would not yield. Dādāsāheb therefore bestowed the title *Samsher Bahādur* on him, and formed an alliance with him. He then went to Gujerat and from thence returned home (to Poona).

The demands issued from Satara on the *Senāpati* remained overdue in spite of repeated expeditors. As it was rumoured that the *Sarkār* intended effecting changes in the office of the *Subha*, the *Senāpati* sent all the (*Sarkār*) messengers to Bānde. Bānde therefore besieged Surat with great determination, to gain either the *takht* or to die. Pilāji Bāba carried it successfully and Bānde expended the proceeds partly in repaying the debt and partly on personal matters. The real balance due from the *Mahāl*, was transferred to the men who came (from Satara) with the demands. Two or three *lākhs* of Rupees were thus paid up. There was further no balance in hand, he (Bānde) promised payment but no cash was forthcoming. The *varātvālās* (agents of Satara) began giving trouble. It was therefore decided that Pilājirāv be deputed with *hundis* worth ten *lākhs* on the *Sardār* of Talegāv and the *Sarkār* be requested to write off the balance. At this juncture Pilāji died of high fever. The *Varatvālās* remained quiet considering the calamity. Damāji Gāikvād was already in service. He had carried on expeditions and successfully achieved some negotiations. Seeing that he was a wise man and a man of action, Bānde conferred the (vacant) post on him and sent him to Dābhāde (the *Senāpati*). He explained matters, but that made no impression on Dābhāde. As the debt amounted to two crores and the cash offered after a long interval did not exceed 10 to 15 *lākhs*, he would not accept the terms. Then Damāji replied, "Agents have to carry out the orders of their masters. I therefore beg you will accept this compromise. If not, the men remain dunning for payment already with my master (Bānde). He will pay in proportion to his income. If this be not acceptable let the Sarkār please itself." He repeated the same answer for a month or two. There was no alternative. When Dābhāde saw this, he advised him (Damāji) to go to Satara and speak to the *Sarkār* (the Mahārāja) and to settle the matter direct. He earnestly begged the favour of not being handed over to the *Sarkār*. "The Balance against us does not amount to 2 crores. It may come up to 60 or 70 *lākhs* of Rupees. Our objections may be considered, and a settlement arrived at. That is a better course. It does not seem (to me) to be the correct way to settle the matter—if I were to pay all demands put forward." After scrutiny, a memo. was drawn, showing about 1 *crore* of Rupees as the actual balance due. Damāji replied that having no territory in his charge he was helpless at seeing such a balance shown. Fifty to sixty *lākhs* seemed to be the real balance due. Even out of that sum deductions would have to be made for insolvent debtors and for the reduced revenue of the *Mahāl*. Then the balance could be recovered by instalments. On this, he was again told to go to Satara. He said he was willing to repay as proposed by him, and asked for a letter of introduction, adding that he would there repeat his request (for compromise). He was then despatched with the dunners (*tagāde*) and *hujrās* (personal staff). Damāji (with the connivance of the *hūjrās*) saw the agents of Dābhāde at Satara. He explained the position to them. The *Sarkār* replied that when the amount due from Dābhāde exceeds 2½ or 3 *crores* how could His Majesty consent to (such a) settlement? The *Sarkār* was requested to do justice. "We shall not demur." The *Sarkār* imposed a fine on Damāji. Damāji took the help of Yamāji Pant and (through him) saw Shripatrāv Pratinidhi. He explained matters to him (Shripatrāv). He showed that including all items such as *Mahāl*-proceeds and expeditions the total amounted only to 85 *lākhs* of Rupees. It was not fair to throw the whole burden on Bānde.

At last all the *Kārbhāris* decided in consultation, that if Dābhāde accepted a lower sum he would not brook alteration of the figure. They therefore proposed a general settlement. Mahārāja was ill at that time. Noticing the scarcity of cash, he (Mahārāja) said that they could accept the terms they thought reasonable. The whole responsibility was therefore thrown on Damāji's head. Damāji replied that he was a mere agent (*vakil*). "His Highness' dunners have seen what amount can be paid on behalf of Bānde. If approved of, the matter may be settled as they (the *Kārbhāris*) decided. I shall submit my request, beyond that I have no power." Then Yamāji Pant said "The debt amounts to 2½ or 3 *crores* and you say that there was no realizations. If each item were to be checked, it would involve loss of time. The *Sarkār* has waited for five or six years. I therefore agree to write off fifty *lākhs* of rupees. If there were no realizations how are you going to pay off Rupees two and half *crores*?" Damāji (Gāikavād) replied, "Dābhāde is the master. You are taking no steps to recover the amount from him and throw the whole burden on my head. I am but a servant of Bānde. I am not responsible for the whole affair." On their deciding what amount is due from him direct, Rupees one *crore* were deducted on his (Dābhāde's) behalf. He was asked to pay off 1½ *crores* the balance then left. Damāji replied that the "real balance against him would be sixty *lākhs* of rupees. Say what you will write off, out of that sum, and accept the balance. I lay this request before the *Senāpati* as well as the *Sarkār*." It was then settled with the approval of the *Pant*, that Damāji should be appointed to the *Subha* and be made *Sena Khāskhel*. Damāji should be held responsible for the debt. All the *Kārbhāris* agreed to this proposal and the order was passed. Damāji accepted the terms and tendered sureties for Rupees forty *lākhs*. The balance was to be paid by instalments. Damāji received the dress (of appointment) and went to Gujerat. Yamāji Pant's and Damāji Bāba's proposals succeeded. The Mahārāja then died. Rājāram Sāheb was adopted. There was trouble among the Kārbhāris. The Peshva and Govindrāv Chitnis formed one party and the *Āi Sāheb* (Queen Dowager) and Yamāji formed the other. But the Peshva had an army under his command. It was decided that the Queen mother and Yamāji should carry on the administration and punish the Peshva. As an army was necessary, Damāji was asked to come with *his* army. There was a battle between him and Nāna Peshva. The names of the principals were suppressed. The Peshva asked Visāji Pant the *Subha* of Bassein to take possession of the Gāikavād's territory. He took the fort of Pārnel. When Bālāji Basvant's brother heard of this, he collected all his *sardārs* and held a consultation and decided that if he were to neglect, the Peshva would take his territory. He would not then be able to defend himself. He therefore decided that the Peshva's army should be punished. He then organized the defence of Songad and Navasari; gave battle to the *Subha* of Bassein and defeated him. Basavant looted the equipage. The Subhedār ran away to save his life. On the other hand Nāna Peshva treacherously arrested Damāji in spite of his own promise. He arrested Rāmchandra Yasvant the *Kārbhāri*, and sent him to Lohagad. Fattesing and Govindrāv Gāikavād were both taken prisoners. They were handed over to Chitnis on his standing security. Damāji was a prisoner for three years. Rāmchandra Basvant promised that he would escape, collect an army, and relieve Damāji, but he ran away to meet Bālāji.

Both the brothers combined, collected an army, and conjointly carried on an expedition. They captured the *Mahāl* officers of the Peshvās, Sindes, and Holkers, imprisoned them, and collected ransoms. The news reached the Peshvas and Damāji's brother came down to Malva. Basvant created trouble in Bāglān, Malhār Rāv did the same in Gujerat. There was trouble on all sides. The Peshvās became restless. Such was the time. (The Peshvās) therefore brought about alliance with Damāji. He was promised half of the territory he might conquer. He was asked to attend himself on the Peshvās at Poona with 5,000 strong. Even if he were to bring more men he was promised expenses. He was made *Se..a Khāskhel Samsher Bahādur* and the *Subha* of Gujerat. He gained success, conquered the Mevāsis and established order. He gave a document announcing the release of Dabhai but Kedārji Gāikavād did not accept it. Therefore Bālāji Rāmchandra Basvant went there and took the fort and distributed the commands of the *Thanas*. They worked together in this way. Dābhāde's connection had already been severed, and an alliance formed between the Peshvās and the Gāikavād.

Damāji became covetous and began studying alchemy. Damāji therefore lived in an obscure village. He was afraid that (his enemies) would take away his wealth and his family would have to beg. One Moslem

Fakir used to make gold. Damāji heard of it, and called the man to him. He was fed and offered a small room for his alchemic experiments. They manufactured gold on three or four occasions and got 5 to 10 *tolās* of it on each occasion. Seeing that, Damāji got a big furnace and bought mercury, arsenic, etc., and personally worked the bellows. As soon as smoke rose out of the furnace, the *fakir* left under the pretext of going to W. C. Damāji closed the door from inside and was suffocated to death. On the next morning people looked and saw that he had breathed his last. His younger son performed his obsequies. Fattesing arrived subsequently. Govindrāv was away in his native place. Sayājirāv was at Baroda. Things happened in this way. Govindrāv wanted to secure the seniority. He saw the *Srimant*, borrowed money from Tāmbekar and Vānavale, collected an army, appointed Tāmbekar his Kārbhāri, took Khando Āvaji with him, and came to Gujerat. Murārāv Gāikavād and Kanhoji Gāikavād remained at Baroda with Sayāji Gāikavād.

Fattesing did not allow Govindrāv to establish himself. There was a battle. Sinde (Pātelbāva) passed through Kolvan, but they could not do so through the Gāikavād territory. Sinde was thus put under fear. Khando Āvaji went to Gwalior, to Gokul, to Vrindavan and then went to his native land. As there was no opportunity to speak to Sinde, Govindrāv went to Poona and stayed there. Nāna Phadnis held out false hopes, accepted bribe from Fattesing, and created trouble. Khando Āvaji died. . Govindrāv found Rāvji Appāji a very honest man, borrowed money through him from the Gosain money-lenders and conducted the duties of the *Sardārship*. After Fattesing's death, Mānāji arrested Yādav Bhāskar and carried on the duties himself but he suffered from syphilis and died within ten months.

Then Nāro Shripat and Govind Vishvanāth went to negotiate debt in their own names. They met Rāvji Appāji. He promised faithful transactions, took him to Govindrāv, and swore by the *bel bhandār*. He got *hundis*, and began negotiations through Haripant Phadke and showed that the financial arrangement was reliable. Nāna said that "the Marāthās (by caste) are dishonest and selfish. The estate has relapsed to *Sarkār* but I have to return it for your sake. You are the keeper and administrator thereof." After due assurances, it was decided that (Govindrāv) should be offered the office, and the dress was given in the fair half of the month of *Bhādrapad*. For two years he was exempted from service and the Peshvās were to help him in establishing his control. The expenses of his help should be repaid within specified time. A document to this effect was drawn up and then was the dress given. Govindrāv left for Baroda. As soon as Mānāji died, Kānhoji Gāikavād undertook the management and remained at Baroda.

DOCUMENT No. 53.

To

R. R. Andora Anna,

From

Rāvji Appāji.

Dated 18th Moon Mohoram (?)

(After compliments.) I am well at Poona and received the letters you sent addressed to Sāvant and Raghoji Patel. I sent Chilo Patel and two peons with a letter to the *Chhatrapati Mahārāja* before yours (under reply) reached me. They must have reached now. After the receipt of your letter Nārāyan *Jāsud* and one *Kānada* peon have been despatched on Saturday with letters to *Shrimant* Mahārāja and *Rājeshri* Lingapa. They also must have reached, and handed over the letters to Lingapa. He must have written the reply he may have received. If not, please write.

At present *Shrimant* Daulatrāv Sinde has written a letter to the Mahārāja about me. I also have written a letter to the Mahārāja. Both the letters have been placed in one envelope and (I have) added a letter to Lingapa. That has been enclosed in the envelope of the letter addressed to you. As soon as you get that letter and the one addressed to the Mahārāja, go to Sātara with Raghoji Patel, see Lingapa, give him his letter, and submit the one addressed to the Mahārāja through him. Repeat the request you communicated to me. "I have no money, and I am neither a thief nor an ungrateful man. And yet, Mahārāja may take all that I possess. But His Highness will see who suffers in reputation. (I have) rendered humble services for forty years. To what extent I have suffered may be considered. Now the self-illuminating sun has risen in the shape of Your Highness. It should destroy the darkness of my poverty." That is left aside and instead (of it) Mahārāja demands money from me! But in his house there is no balance standing against me. His Highness is by nature extravagant and luxurious and is therefore in debt to the extent of *lākhs* of Rupees. That is true. I will swear as to its truth by any sacred thing (Mahārāja names). Submit a clear request like this.

Andoba! Mahārāja has, under displeasure, harassed all people. May that please him. He is the father and mother (of us all). Tell Lingapa that I will not pay a single rupee as fine. Let him do what he thinks just and fair. Bāpu Bhatt has been detained because he has incurred some debt at Wāi and wants more money for the house. Money has not yet been obtained. Within a day or two I shall try to get one or two thousand and despatch the sum to him. Sāvant and Raghoji Patel belong to the Shiledār's family. I keep you informed of it.

Andoba Anna! You write as if you are afraid. But I cannot help it. Bāpu Bhatt will explain matters. What more to write? Be kind is my request.

Despatched on the 20th of *Mohoram*.

DOCUMENT No. 54.

Chronicle.

Under *Shrimant Chhatrapati* Shivāji Mahārāj, was employed Prayāg Anant Phanse resident of Panvel. He was wise, clever, a good writer and a good speaker. He was at the head of the Konkanes and Māvals. The Mahārāja was pleased to appoint him *Subhedār* of forts Satara and Parali (*Shak* 1607).

* * * *

Prayāg Bāva was given the command of the fort of Satara and installed as the head of the *Gadakaris* (guards of the fort). Prayāgji Bāva was present at four or five battles fought against the Moghals. He was successful.

He married twice. The elder wife had four sons. Of these Antāji Prayāg was the eldest. The second wife had also four sons. Their names will be given in due course. Antāji Prayāg had four sons. The eldest was Jyoti Anant, the second was Laxman Anant, the third Kāshirāv Anant and the fourth Mahipatrāv. Jyoti Anant had four sons. The eldest was Gangādhar Jyoti, the second, Chimnāji Jyoti, the third, Bhāskar Jyoti *alias* Rāvji Appāji, the fourth was Rakhmāji Jyoti *alias* Bābāji Appāji.

In *Shak* 1608 Emperor Aurangzeb came from Delhi. He captured Sambhāji Mahārāja. Everything was in confusion. Rājārām Sāheb was thinking of going to Chandi. At this time the Manglāi bastion of the fort was blown up by the Emperor after placing explosives under its foundation. The siege was in full force. The bastion was blown up. It rose like a kite to about 150 or 200 feet. Soldiers guarding the bastion were thrown out by the force and killed on the spot. Some were wounded. The *Subhedār* was also blown up and lay buried in the debris. But he was not much hurt. The siege lasted until the evening. Tired soldiers returned to their quarters. At night, *Kārkuns* and soldiers were despatched with torches to investigate the loss. On the third morning a portion of the dress of the *Subhedār* attracted attention. On hallooing, it was found that he was still alive. He was taken out (by the grace of God). Mahārāja was pleased to find him alive. He was asked to name a reward. He said that villages may be granted him in the vicinity of the temple he had built. *Mauje* Kalambe was granted as a perpetual gift. Some land was also granted at Chinchner-Dehegāv. They are still in the enjoyment of the family. Prayāgji acquired a great reputation in this manner. After some years Nānāsāheb Peshvā began administering the State. He was succeeded by Mādhavrāv Ballāl. With him there were Sakhārām Bāpu Bokil and Bāburāv Phadnis. During that time Bhāskar Jyoti *alias* Rāvji Appāji was entrusted with the duty of negotiations, as he was liked by all and was acquainted with many *raises* and *ryots*. Whenever any disputed cases came before the *Sarkār*, Rāvba was selected for the reconciliation of the disputants as he was a straightforward and honest man. Every year he had to deal with five or six such complicated cases. After due enquiry Rāvba used to report the case to the *Sarkār* and carry out the orders (of the *Sarkār*) and recover fines. He thus added a few rupees to the income of the State. Officers were pleased with him. In this manner Rāvba became a favourite of the *Darbār*.

Men who were employed to negotiate on behalf of Govindrāv Gāikavād could not succeed; and although he was the senior, he could not get the orders and dress of the office (of Gāikavād) because Mānājirāv, Fattesing Rāv and Sayāji Bāba had not offered substantial *Nazars* and tribute. There was no decision and they had no intelligent and influential agent at the *Darbār*. Their father Damāji Rāv Gāikavād had died at Pattan. At that time, Govindrāv Bāba was on duty at Poona. When he heard of it, he offered the usual *Nazar* to the *Sarkār*, received the dress, recovered the *Nazars*, and *rasads*, due from the Māmledārs of his state, paid 20,00,000 (twenty *lākhs* of rupees) into the state treasury. He took his cavalry and army, established his power by despatching Māmledārs in accordance with the custom. He captured Fort Songad. Before he could proceed, Fattesing Bāba came to Poona and opened negotiations through Gopāl Nāik Tāmbekar and got two *sanads*, one in his own name, and another in Govindrāv's name. One of them was for the office of the *Senākhāskhel*, and the other for *Samasher Bahādur*. It was decided that the acceptance of the duty of each section be left to their choice. Govindrāv Bāva accepted the *Samshersardārship*. The *Sena khās-khelship* was given to Fattesing. He accepted it and left for Gujerat. Amin

Sāheb 's(?) father Hamid Miyya was there (?). with his army. Govindrāv Bāba's army came to that place (?) from Songad. They fought a battle. In that battle Chimnāji Jyoti of Kalambe was killed. Rāvba Bāba went there and performed his obsequies. Fattesing arrived there with power to administer the state. Govindrāv 's army was sent back.

After this, Govindrāv Bāva used to see the *Shrimant* (Peshva), with Mahādji Sinde and Māloji Rāje Ghorpade, and tell them that as Fattesing Bāva was entrusted with the internal administration of the state, Govindrāv Bāba was obliged to remain at Pocna on (Military) duty. Fattesing Rāv had been making no arrangement for his expenses and the Māmledārs he (Govindrāv) had deputed to the *Mahāl* to recover the *Nazar* paid by him, had been sent back (by Fattesing). How was he to maintain himself ? (The Peshva) said " The district belonged to (troublesome) Mewāsis, they will pay later on. If he (Fattesing) takes time, what is the use of quarrelling? That is not proper." He (Peshva) told Gopāl Nāik to refund the amount (of the *Nazar*) paid (by Govindrāv) and get the orders back. The *Shrimant* (Peshva) went to Karnatak in *Samvat* 1828. Govindrāv accompanied him, and so did Dādāsāheb Peshvā. They invaded the territory of the Moghal, and Govindrāv proved useful with his army of 10,000 strong. Dādāsāheb therefore found him a brave man and was favourably impressed. Dādāsāheb was imprisoned by Rāvsāheb (Mādhavrāv) Peshvā. In *Shak* 1694, *Samvat* 1828 Rāvsāheb died. Nārāyanrāv became Peshvā. Dādāsāheb went out on an expedition against the Moghals. He conquered a territory yielding 20 *lākhs* a year. Then Nārāyanrāv got into trouble. That history about Sumersing *Gārdi* has already been recorded in the chronicle about the Peshvās. Then Dādāsāheb went to Dhar. At that place *Shrimant*

Bājirāv was born with the face towards the earth! Then Govindrāv went to Gujerāt with Patel Bāva, Sinde. The Māmledārs returned to Gujerat with the army. They came back and sat *dharna* on Khando Āvaji to represent Gabāji and the *Kārbhāri*. They would not allow him to leave his place. When he went to the tent, no one was allowed to enter it or to come out of it. At that time Rāvji Appāji went to enquire after his health, but there was a disturbance and he could not see him (Khando). He (Rāvji) enquired and escaping the notice of the guard entered the tent. He asked Govindrāv "What would happen if the news of this disturbance about debt reaches the *Shrimant*?" After protesting in this manner in several ways, he came out (of the tent) and threatened the agents of the creditors and said "What will you get by enforcing such a dunning? When the master is installed on his *gādi*, arrangements will be made for the payment." He explained matters in different ways. In this manner Rāvba saved Govindrāv from a critical position involving death. Govindrāv (Gāikavād) felt much indebted and always remembered it.

Govindrāv Gāikavād tried through Pātil Bāva and the *Darbāris* to get charge of Gujerāt. Mādhavrāv Peshvā was applied to, but he asserted that he would not change what he had once said. On that, Govindrāv went to Hindustan with Pātil Bāva (Sinde). At that time Khando Āvaji requested Rāvba to help him with money and assured him that he (Govindrāv) would not succeed in raising a loan without his (Rāvba's) help. Rāvba said "On what grounds shall I stand security for him?" Khando Āvaji said "*Sardār* Govindrāv is your master because your brother Chimnāji Jyoti is his servant. You are therefore his servant in a way. And, besides, he is your friend. You have helped him several times, now he is helpless as regards the loan. This cannot be managed without you." Rāvba replied "I am not a monied man. I am doing my best. You know it. Nobody would work without money. Why do you try me in this way?" Then Tāmbekar added "I have three or four times opened the subject with the Nāik. He consented if a security be offered. He asked us to find out a security. On this it was settled that Bhide should advance Rupees fifty thousand to one *lākh.* The document was tendered and the amount received. It was promised that the amount would be refunded on his (Govindrāv's) going to Gujerāt and Bhide added that Rāvba should accompany him (Govindrāv) to Gujerāt and remit the amount as stipulated. The question of appointing Khandopant was under consideration, but this was a better arrangement as it emanated from Bhide. Pant was glad. Bābāsāheb was informed of these facts and told how the matter was settled. After that, hearing that Dādāsāheb was coming (to Poona) with the help of the English, Sinde and Haripant went out to meet them. They met near Navasari on the banks of the Narbada. Dādāsāheb went to Surat as soon as the battle began. In obedience to orders from Calcutta a European army of four regiments went to Talegāv through Borghāt. There was a battle. The chief commandant was Istur *Phākda.* He was killed. The English army returned to Bombay. Eight villages out of the Salsette group were given away to Dādāsāheb and peace was concluded. The villages were handed over to Dādāsāheb. They (the army?) were kept at Koregāv.

Rāvji Appāji was a favourite of the *Shrimant* (Peshvā) and of the *Kārbhāris.* He was kindly treated, was given job-work. He was thus enabled to earn his livelihood. Rāvba on the other hand worked very scrupulously, and maintained the supremacy of the Peshvās. At this time Chimnāji Jyoti came there with Govindrāv Gāikavād. After receiving the dress of honour of the *Sardārship*, he recovered money—the amount recorded by the *Māmledārs* as "District charges." To establish his reign he sent portions of his army with the *Māmledārs*. When he (Rāvba) prepared to go to Gujerāt, he was asked (by Chimnāji) "Why are you going? We shall live in peace with half the bread left to us by our ancestors." Govindrāv told him "This we should consider as *our* family work. You and I are not separate. Do not be anxious. I am yours in all respects. Let him go." At such a homely request, he consented. He (Rāvba) was sent. Fattesingrāv then came (to Poona) and got his "*Mulki* Command." A battle took place near Songad and a few men were killed. Chimnāji Jyoti was also killed, on the battlefield. When Rāvba heard of this he was very sorry. Govindrāv tried to console him in many ways. When Rāvba returned to Gujerāt after working with Sinde and Dādāsāheb, and gaining their good opinion, Govindrāv went forward to receive him and informed him of what had happened. On moving the *Sāheb* at Surat through Dādāsāheb, permission was received to invade Baroda. The *Sāheb* was to take Princess Vārābāi the daughter of Fattesingrāv as a hostage and to establish order at Baroda. But Sinde and Holkar marched with their artillery against Dādāsāheb. That produced great disturbance and the *Sāheb* took hostages. Fattesing paid some money and formed alliance with the English. It was stipulated that they (the English) should not side with Govindrāv. After that, Haripant was entertained. Govindrāv went to Poona. Even Pātil Bāva found it difficult to negotiate matters with Mādhavrāv Nārāyan the Peshvā and Nāna and Haripant the *Kārbhāris*. Rāvba had free access to the *Darbār*. Govindrāv therefore secured his friendship and through him swore alliance with Pātil Bāva. Keeping that in mind, he used to repeat the assurance but Rāvba had to work in conformity with the wishes of the *Darbār*. He therefore pulled on well. Nilkanthrāv Pāge (Commandant of the Cavalry) Māloji Ghorpade and Mānāji Fākde interested themselves (in this case) and spoke to the Peshvā. On the other hand, the *Pātil* of Deccan-Hyderabad spoke on behalf of Govindrāv. He was friendly with the *Sāheb-lok.* He therefore used to tell them the purport. Govindrāv spoke to Nāna and Haripant about this matter many a time. He was told that Rāvba should not trouble them on this subject, because on account of his partisanship of Dādāsāheb, there was some prejudice against him. That is why no definite reply was given (by the Peshvā). He should understand this and keep quiet. After that, Fattesingrāv died in *Suru San tissa Samanin.* Mānāji became the chief. From that moment Rāvba again commenced speaking to Nāna on this matter. Nāna was very kind to Rāvba. He therefore did not give an unfavourable decision, but only said "Why are you anxious? You will get some good appointment from the *Sarkār.*" This state continued for a long time. At last Rāvba said that Govindrāv was living at Poona for a long time at daily expense. "My brother died fighting for him. On that account he (Govindrāv) came to me. He has been eating and fasting on alternate days. When he comes to my house, there is no alternative but that of relieving him. Whenever he is annoyed by his creditors, he sends for me and gets me entangled in the affair, and the creditors kindly listen to me and go back. On this account I am much involved. It is hoped that the *Sarkār* will make him the master of Gujerāt to relieve me from my promise. If I (Rāvba) am entrusted with *Sarkār*-service, I shall take Govindrāv (Gāikavād) to Baroda, and will arrange for the repayment of the balance due from him. I will show that I can render valuable services. But do confer on him this favour," Rāvba further learnt that the news of the demise of Mānāji had reached that *Sarkār*. At this time Govind Vishvanāth wrote to Nāna that "the *Sardārship* (of Gujerat) has no master and *Sarkār* has to recover heavy dues. It may therefore be resumed and handed over to him for administration. I shall pay such and such amount as *Nazar*." But before that, Nāro Shripati had submitted a proposal on behalf of Mānāji Rāv. When the agent (of Nāro Shripati) was going to a middle-man with *hundis*, a friend of Rāvba read them. Rāvba asked him to show him these papers and ascertained that they referred to the dress announcing the appointment. He told them to accompany him. He took them to Govindrāv and (in his presence) explained the day of the demise of Mānāji. He assured them of the fact, took them thence to Haripant Tātia and proposed that Govindrāv be (now) offered the dress. Tātia replied, "Yes, you have been speaking about this proposal for a long time. It is true. I remember it, but how to succeed without money? What to do for that? This is the opportunity. Mānāji is dead. You can now speak on the subject." He (Rāvba) promised to pay in proportion, to the best of his power and added that if he (Tātia) interests himself there was hope of success. "You will (I hope) interest yourself." Tātia replied "When was I not interested? You have been arranging for (the money) ever since Fattesing's death. When proposals about Mānāji were opened, he was told (to produce cash). He died before he could do so. Your proposal is still under consideration." Rāvba replied "If you tell me to-day that you will interest yourself and obtain the desired decision, I will arrange for the payment. I will not leave your house until I do so on the spot." Tātia replied "In, what way will you arrange for the cash?" Rāvba replied "If you mention a modest sum I can pay at this moment and if you wish to refuse there is no help." Then Tātia replied, "Pay one year's income as a *nazar* in addition to the *Darbār Kharch* (payments to Darbār officers). Tell me how you propose repaying the balance." Rāvba replied, "Settle the amount of the year's income, and the payments to the *Darbāris*, and then I will speak about the balance. Do what you think proper, in consideration of the loss suffered during the last twenty years. We have no support except yourself." He replied "Rāvba! You are mine and I am yours, but the debt is due to the *Sarkār*, unless it is paid how am I to speak to the *Sarkār*? Unless therefore the 'personal' terms with Tātia were settled and the *Darbār's* expenses are fixed in consultation with Nāna he (Tātia) would not speak. He was shown a bill of exchange for sixty *lākhs* of rupees. He was asked to come back in the evening to accompany him to Nāna's house to settle that day all final details. Then he (Rāvba) was introduced to Gopālji Gundo the *Khijamatgār* (A.D.C.) of Nāna. He informed Nāna. Nāna replied, "Why does Rāvba work in such matters? *Sarkār* wishes to employ him as Nyāyādhish (Chief Justice). What is the surety of the promises of the Marāthas by caste (meaning the Gāikavād's tribe). He trusts them and gets himself involved. This is not good." On this Gopālji Gundo said "Rāvji Appāji has been pulling on under your protection during these twenty years. He works in obedience to your advice. He never accepts any bribe in doing that work. It is not because his family people have been complaining (of want of support). They say "Why do you get yourself into trouble over Govindrāv's affairs. We shall live on our own income. If there were any additional income from outside, there would have been no objection. That you do not get and waste your time." Such is the way in which his brothers speak to him. I heard it. All that Rāvba could earn and get on credit has been devoted to Govindrāv. He will not give up that 'monomania,' all the days of his life until he is weaned from that affair, that is, his connection with Govindrāv as contracted in some preceding birth. He must have owed him (Govindrāv) some heavy debt in a former birth. As somebody will have to be deputed to the Gāikavād to arrange for the recovery of the debt due, he (Rāvba) may be told off to do that duty—after ascertaining how he arranges for the securities of the repayment. If he does not do so satisfactorily he may not be employed." Nāna heard all this and remained silent.

Then about 8 o'clock at night Haripant Tātia took Rāvba with him and went to Nāna's house. He opened the subject. He said, "Rāvba waited so long, because he did not want to create trouble while matters were running smooth, and Fattesing and Mānāji were working on the spot. They were well informed, they had the land in their possession. There was no profit to the Government if they were made to spend money in establishing order. Now they are both dead and have left no heirs. Govindrāv has a son there (in Gujerat) and therefore our state should be handed over to us. The dress of honour of the *Sardārship* may now be kindly presented again and we may be sent there on behalf of the *Sarkār*." After this Nāna discussed one or two more points regarding the proposal to resume and to hold the land direct. Tātia said "that it would be difficult to resume the state. That was not a good proposal. We must arrange for some scheme in which the state can be handed over to Govindrāv."

Nāna replied, "No services were rendered to the state, although such a service formed the condition, and the fixed amount of ransom has not been paid. There is still standing a heavy balance. Govindrāv will not be able to bear the weight of these responsibilities and no appointment can be made until the balance is paid. Then tell me in what way do you propose to proceed? Your proposals will then receive consideration." Tātia asked, "To whom was the first payment about the dress made? To Govindrāv or to Fattesing? Look at the accounts, strike a balance and we shall submit proposals for its settlement." Account papers were obtained from the *Guruji*. On examining them it was found that there was a heavy balance. Then Haripant Tātia said, "We cannot settle the whole affair to-day. Let the work be done departmentally. (I think) We should accept one year's income as *Nazar* and depute *Huzrās* to recover the balance." A memo. was drawn up in accordance. Haripant undertook to guarantee the payment of instalments and it was settled that the dress of honour announcing the appointment be given the next day. They were working with this scheme until midnight. Then they returned under the protection of the guard, who controlled traffic at night in conformity with the regulations of the "Curfew" Bell-like gun.

The dress was to be given the next day, but 14 *Mahāls* of the 28 constituting the Surat province were handed over to the *Nabāb*. Out of the remaining 14, seven were to be resumed by the Peshvās and only seven to be handed over to the Gāikavād. When it was given out that the 7 *Mahāls* were to be resumed, Rāvba could not undertake to convey the news, because he was the Minister-elect and he would suffer in the estimation of his chief. When therefore Mānāji Gāikavād was alive one Svarupräm Munshi was employed as a spy to watch and report what Govindrāv was doing. He was now employed at the *Bet* under Mallet *Sāheb*. After Mānāji's demise he lived with Govindrāv as a flatterer. He said, that there existed an agreement in which the British undertook to help the Gāikavād if the Peshvā or any other power interfered with his dominion. He asserted that he knew it for certain. He suggested that if this matter were referred to Mallet *Sāheb*, the *Kārbhāris* (of Poona) would not have to say anything. He went to Mallet *Sāheb* and informed him that "after deciding that Govindrāv be appointed Gāikavād, the (Peshvā) now says that he will be given the requisite dress only if he hand over Navsari *Mahāls*. You (Mallet *Sāheb*) have agreed to help if there be any dispute about land. There is a *Bahādari* (guarantee) to that effect and suggested that he should say "There is nothing to be said if it is really handed over willingly. If it be resumed forcibly that will not do."

(He added) "You say that, and he (Govindrāv) will be given the dress. Unless you speak in an assertive tone, this thing will not be done." On hearing this he (Mr. Mallet) consented, went to the Peshvā and asked "Has the question of the Gāikavād of Gujerat been settled or not?" Nāna asked him in return "Why do you put such a question?" He replied "There is an agreement between us (the British) and the Gāikavād and we have undertaken to help him. That we shall not allow any power to interfere with his territory." He (Mr. Mallet) then added "that the question be settled and he be allowed to go. This was a friendly request."

On account of this speech, the proposal of resuming Navasari was dropped. *Payment to Haripant* (*Phadke*) was settled through Krishnambhat Patvardhan, his family priests. *Nāna's affair* (payment) was settled by Tatia (Haripant Phadke) and he arranged for the ceremony of giving the dress in a *Darbār*. When Govindrāv started (in procession) to receive the dress, he was supplied with retainers by Nilkanthrāv Pāgé (Commandant). They consisted of horses duly caparisoned and adorned with gold and silver ornaments, camel *sawārs* and elephant cavalry. Māloji Rāje Ghorpade supplied mounted guards. About seven or eight hundred attendants were thus supplied. Govindrāv had two elephants of his own. With these and with his own horses, drum bearers and flags, Govindrāv was escorted to the *wāda* (Peshva's house) and was received by Nāna and Haripant. He was offered a seat near the *gādi* (masnad).

All those who were friendly to Govindrāv were speaking to the *Sarkār*. Seeing that he was in financial difficulty they urged that he should be helped. Among them Pātil Bāva was very earnest. He was an intimate friend of Haripant (Phadke). When therefore Haripant referred to Dādāsāheb's treason he (Sinde) replied that Govindrāv only spoke about the *Sardārship*. "He has done no harm to the *Sarkār* (and added) that he knew it well. For the sake of the 'belly' one may serve anybody." This was done at Rāvba's suggestion and Sinde spoke to Nāna accordingly. Nāna therefore said that he did not entertain any unfavourable opinion on that account. When they stopped speaking the *Vakil* of the Mongals said "Nimbālkar was asked to look into the question of the loss his master's territory had to suffer and when you have no *Sardār* in Gujerat, how is it that Govindrāv goes about styling himself a Rāja. Why does the *Sarkār* not take notice of that? He was told that at the time the treaty was framed it was proposed that the "Surat Aththāvisi" province should be handed over to the *Sarkār*. But from the *sāheblok*-side it was arranged that if anybody were to interfere with the treaty so arranged with Fattesing they would help him. A message was received from them (*sāheblok*) that "if any proposals were made in contravention of that treaty they would be forced to help him (the Gāikavād). There are written documents extant on the subject." At this reply Nāna felt constrained, and it was decided that Govindrāv be offered the appointment. He was thereafter given the dress of honour of the *Sardārship*.

When he offered the dress of the *Divānship* to Rāvba, Nāna said to Govindrāv that "Rāvji was a hereditary servant of the *Sarkār*. I transfer him to you because he worked hard for you with the *Sarkār*. Administer your state under his counsel. Repay the debt you owe to the *Sarkār*. *Sarkār-huzras* will be told off to do that work." The dress was ceremoniously given after such remarks. After receipt of the dress Govindrāv returned home and distributed alms among Brahmans and fed them with sweets. The usual reception was held and clothes presented as usual. When it was known that Govindrāv received the *khillāt* for Baroda, many people came to see him. Some were Govindrāv's friends and some were Rāvba's friends or friends' friends. Many wanted to go to Baroda and many were the recommendations received. Direct refusal would have produced discontent and it was not advisable to give an opportunity to people to grumble—while living in the capital. Everyone was therefore courteously told that "he (Govindrāv) has suffered great loss during the recent interval. All know it well. After reaching Baroda and establishing himself, he would consider the claims of every applicant. It was not possible to arrange for their departure, because there was no cash in hand." Those therefore who wanted to go forthwith were asked to finance their own expenses and told that they should not reopen the question until he (Govindrāv) reached his capital. After everything was settled, arrangement was to be made in accordance with demand for men and the income of the state. In this manner Rāvba managed the affair and informed Bābāsāheb (Govindrāv) of what he did. Govindrāv remarked that the whole state was at Rāvba's disposal. "I will eat only what you would give me. You need not take my permission to manage these affairs. Still in due deference as a servant, he kept him (Govindrāv) daily informed of what he was doing. They started with Mādhavrāv Gopāl Karandikar, Krishnarāv Bhat Patvardhan, Nawāb Mir Kamāluddin, Māloji Rāje Ghorpade's mistress, Mohan Rāni, and her son, including seven or eight officers entitled to palanquins. There were besides many respectable Brahmans *Sāwkārs*, *Bhāts*, *Bhikshuks*, *Marāthas* (by caste) and Prabhus—among the latter figured Balvantrāv Kāshi Phanse, Vithal Yashvant Potnis, Sadāshiv Laxman, Chitnis Govindrāv, Bhāi 'Jevlia,' Hari Rāv, Mukund Jagoba Dāda, Nilkanthrāv Pāgé's nephew his brother Bhikoba. There were besides many Marātha *shiledārs* and Konknes.

When Govindrāv parted from Pātil Bāva, Khando Āvji died on the way. Govindrāv was very sorry. He embraced Rāvba and said "Up to this time you and Khandopant were working conjointly for me. But now I have no faithful adherent except yourself. You are my sole support, mother, sister, father, brother, kith and kin. I will submit even if you cut my throat. I and my descendants will never neglect you and your descendants. I swear (to that effect) by my father, mother and family gods."

There are many letters on record to the same effect. While Pātil Bāva was with them, Rāvba managed to gain his good opinion, informed him of Bābāsāheb's difficulties and got permission to leave him. He carried on the daily expenses and refunded some part of the amount due to Bhide.

Rāvba then went to Poona. Govindrāv went to Baroda and raised a siege, *Shake* 1693.

After that Dādāsāheb (Raghunāthrāv Peshva) came from Dhar. He met (Govindrāv) at Harnai near Baroda. Govindrāv went (in advance) to see him. Then came the British regiments and Dādāsāheb returned to Surat.

On reaching Barod, Govindrāv found that there was an excess of Arabs in the army. Nothing could be done without them. They ill-treated many people. If a man accidentally stumbled (on any of the Arabs) he was instantly killed. There was no remedy, no complaint and no appeal! Holkor's army and Sinda's army looted (parts of the territory). There was such an anarchy in the state. The troubles caused by the chief of Bhuj (Kachch) and Nagar (Jāmnagar) interfered with the recovery of the revenue of Kathiavad. People were harassed. The Peshva had promised that if there was trouble in the Baroda territory he would settle the matter. He would send an army. Yet Rāvba was recalled to Poona by Rājirav II, to arrange for the repayment of the old balance due. He informed (the Peshva) of the state of affairs at Baroda but was told that "when there was trouble in Poona itself how could the Gāikavād be assisted? You had better manage the state in the best way you yourself can." Receiving such orders, Rāvba went to Banal who had influence with the *Sahebs*. From there he got armies from Mir Kamāluddin and Nawāb *sāheb*, and Gopālrāv and removed Malhārrāv from Kadi to Nadiad. He brought the province of Ahmedabad under control with the co-operation of the *sāhebs*.

Then the *sāhebs* took Cambay and made a treaty. It was found difficult to repay the debt because the Arabs had ruined the state. The *sāhebs* complained. They were told that "the Baroda state counted on the perpetual friendship of the Honourable Company. The *Sena Khaskhel* and his successors and your (English) successors will live in close friendship. What a gain will it be!" Bābāji, Sitārāmji, Sakhāram Divānji and Gopālrāv were deputed to carry this message. Such was the friendship and such is now the state.

APPENDIX.

Govind Rāv Gāikawād.

"Govind Rāo Gaikwār was sent by his father Dummājee to support Rughonāth Rāo, against Māhdoo Rāo, in the rebellion of 1768. Shortly after its suppression Dummājee died leaving four sons, Syājee, Govind Rāo, Mānikjee and Futih Sing. The two last were the youngest and full brothers by the third wife. Syājee was the eldest son, but by Dummājee's second wife. Govind Rāo was his second son, but by the first married wife. * * Govind Rāo was at Poona at the time of his father's death, a 'prisoner at large' in consequence of having supported Rughonāth Rāo. His claim to the succession, and to his father's rank of *Sena Khāskheyel*, does not in the first instance appear to have been disputed. Upon his paying a fine of upwards of twenty-three *lacks* of rupees, for his late delinquency, a *nuzur* of twenty-one *lacks*, and other exactions amounting in all to upwards of fifty *lacks* and a half, and having also agreed to pay a tribute of seven *lacks* and seventy-nine thousand rupees annually, to keep three thousand horse constantly in the service at Poona, and four thousand when the Peishwa was at war, the title and possessions of his father were conferred upon Govind Rāo" (Grant Duff.)

"Govind Rāo presented a petition to the minister, praying to be acknowledged by the Peishwa as regent of the Gāekwār possessions. His claim was just, but Mānnājee Rāo, was by paying a *Nuzur* * * confirmed in his usurpation. Mahādājee Sindia, however, espoused the cause of Govind Rāo and procured a repeal of Mānnājee's appointment, upon which Mānnājee applied to the Bombay Government, claiming its protection on the terms of the treaty conducted with General Goddard by Tulip Sing. As the treaty in question was superseded by that of Salbye, the English declined all interference on that ground, * * but they were induced to recommend, through Mr. Malet, that some friendly compromise should be accepted. * * Nāna Furnuwees concurred in this opinion, but Mahādājee Sindia and the partizans of Govind Rāo, objected to any compromise. The question was, however, at once set at rest by the death of Mānnājee about 1st August 1793. Still Govind Rāo found it difficult to obtain permission to quit the Peishwa's capital. The ministers, without any regard to the exorbitant exactions already imposed on himself and his family, obliged Govind Rāo to sign an agreement confirming the former stipulations, and ceding to the Peishwa the Gāekwar's share of the districts south of the Taptee, formerly included in the cessions to the Company in 1780 together with his proportion of the customs of Surat; but there being no service performed by the Peishwa, towards the Gāekwar, beyond the mere confirmation of his rights as regent, the British Government objected to the cession as a dismemberment of the Baroda territory, contrary to the stipulations of the treaty of Salbye. The validity of this objection was immediately admitted by Nāna Furnuwees, the instrument of cession was restored, and Govind Rāo at last set out to assume his office, as undisputed regent at Baroda, on the 19th December, 1793."[1]

Khando Ballāl Chitnis.

" Khando Ballāl was present at the council of the principal people assembled at Raigad, and declared Rājā-Rām as the regent, after Sambhāji's death.

[1] Grant Duff, Vol. III, pp. 94-95.

"He took a very active part in protecting Rājārām during his flight to Ginjee in disguise. On one occasion the slight circumstance of having Rājārām's feet washed by a servant at first attracted attention. The wary observation of Khando Ballāl discovered that there was a plan for arresting the whole party, and to disappoint the scheme, Khando Ballāl with the majority of the party remained cooking their victuals, while Rāja-Rām and some others went off and escaped. Khando Ballāl (Chitnis) and his companions were taken, as had been foreseen : they were examined, confined and beaten to extort confession but on their firmly persisting in a preconcerted story and denying all knowledge of any fugitives from Mahārāshtra, they were released, and finally joined Rājārām, who with others, had reached Ginjee in safety."[1] Such was the fidelity of Khaṇḍo Ballāl, that he was held in great esteem.

Prayāgji Prabhu.

"The fort which occupies the summit of a very steep hill of moderate height, the defence consisting of a sheer scrap of over forty feet topped by a stone wall, was defended by Prayāgji Prabhu Havildār, who had been reared in the service of Shivāji. He vigorously opposed the Moghals and disputed every foot of ground as they pushed forward their advanced posts. As soon as they began to gain any part of the hill, he withdrew his troops into the fort and rolled huge stones from the rock above, which did great execution, and, until they threw up cover, were as destructive as artillery. In spite of Prayāgji's efforts the blockade was completed !"[2]

"Prayāgji, the Marātha commandant, was buried in the ruins caused by the first explosion close to a temple dedicated to the goddess Bhavāni, but was afterwards

[1] Grant Duff, Vol. I, p. 365.

[2] Grant Duff, Vol. I, pp. 365, 369.

dug out alive. His escape was considered a lucky omen and under other circumstances might have done much to inspirit the garrison to prolong the defence."[1]

Rāoji Appāji, Bābāji Appāji, Sitārām Rāoji, Vithalrāv Bābāji and Bhāskarrāv Vithal the descendants of Prayāgji were Ministers of Baroda. The present scion is Shrimat Dāda Sāheb *alias* Ramchandra Vithalrāv Phanse, Khāsgivāle, the hereditary Tālukdār of Vithalgad in Kāthiawad.

Rājārām Mahārāja.

"Ascends the throne, but some of the Marāthas, jealous of the right of the elder branch, do not admit that Rājārām ever sat on the throne. They say that he sat on the *gādi*, or cushion, merely as regent, holding the powers of the State in trust for his nephew Shāhu (Shāo) then a prisoner in the Moghul camp."[2]

Rāvji Appāji.

(Spelt Rowjee Appajee in Grant Duff's History.)

"He (the rebel Kānhojee Rāo) was deposed by a party headed by Rowjee Appājee, a Purvoe (Prabhu) who was the principal minister of the late Govind-Rāo. Rowjee the minister in power and Kanhojee (the deposed authority) made offers to the Bombay Government. Rowjee was supported by his brother Bābājee. Rowjee's party was the strongest in Baroda. * * * The minister immediately proposed to the Bombay Government to subsidize five battalions. Major Alexander Walker, who was sent as the officer in command of the detachment, was instructed to settle the disturbance by amicable mediation, if possible; otherwise, he was to act with Bābājee in suppressing the rebellion of Mulhār Rāo. * * * Although Rowjee Appājee

[1] Bombay Gazetteer, Vol. XIX, p. 251.

[2] Grant Duff, Vol. I, p. 371.

was anxious for power, and jealous of authority (of the State), he gladly solicited support when insurrections were to be suppressed, the Government to be strengthened, its expenses to be reduced, money to be raised, and debt to be reduced."

"The ministry was chiefly composed of a set of Purvoes, (Prabhus) a cast (*sic*) frequently remarkable for great fidelity and bravery, and when poor, they are often frugal to parsimony, but it may be observed of the Purvoes (Prabhus) that wherever they attain power, and can command wealth they are lavish and improvident. The head of this ministry was Rowjee Appājee who died in July, 1803."[1]

Sakhāram Bāpu.

" Sukārām Bhugwunt Bhokeel, Koolkurnee of Hewra, and the descendant of Puntojee Gopināth, who betrayed Afzool Khan into the hands of Sivājee, was the principal minister at the period when the British Government first took an active part in the politics of the Poona *Darbār*, and is best known by his familiar name Sakārām Bāppoo."

"It is necessary to state that Sukārām Bāppoo was originally concerned in Rāgoba's conspiracy against the liberty, though not the life, of Nārrāin-Rāo. After the murder, as it was deemed by the ministers generally, a measure of prudence to affect a disbelief of Rugonath's participation, of course Sukārām Bāppoo had stronger reasons than any of them, for professing that opinion."

"But Sukārām's death scene was not closed in Pertabgurh, the cautious jealousy of Nāna Furnuwees removed him secretly from one place to another to prevent rescue or insurrection, and once great Sukārām Bāppoo perished miserably in Rāigurh."[2]

[1] Grant Duff, Vol. III.

[2] Grant Duff, Vol. II, p. 397.

Sakhārām Hari.

" His friend (Raghunāthrāv Peshva's) Sakhārām Hari (Sukārām Hurry) who fought by his side, enabled him to defend himself until rescued by his nephew."[1]

(2) " A body of Arabs, whom he had lately entertained, refused to fight without pay, Mānājee Phākray and Sakhārām Hari, two of his best officers, were wounded in the commencement."[2]

(3) " The unshaken constancy of Sakhārām Hari to his master Rāghoba deserved a better fate. He was chained in irons so heavy that, although a very powerful man, he could scarcely lift them; his food and water were insufficient to allay his hunger or to quench his thirst; but he survived fourteen months; and when so emaciated that he could not rise,— " My strength is gone and my life is going," said the dying enthusiast, " but when voice and breath fail, my flesh and bones shall still shout Raghunāth-Rāv! Raghunāth-Rāv! "

" Sakhārām Hari was a Prabhu and is not a singular instance of the unshaken fidelity of that class in the history of Mahārāshtra."[3]

Satara.

The fort of Satara occupies the summit of a hill of moderate height, but very steep; its defences consist of a scrap of upwards of forty feet in perpendicular black rock, on the top of which there is a stone wall. It was defended by Pryāgjee Purvoe (Prayāgji Prabhu), Havildār, who had been reared in the service of Shivājee. He vigorously opposed the Moghuls and disputed every foot of ground as they pushed forward their advanced posts. As soon as they began to gain any part of the hill, he withdrew

[1] Grant Duff, Vol. II, p. 175. [2] Grant Duff, Vol. II, p. 287.
[3] Grant Duff, Vol. II, p. 353.

his troops into the fort, and rolled down huge stones from the rock above, which did great execution, and until they could throw up cover, were as destructive as artillery. The blockade, however, was complete, no communication could be held with the country, and as the small stock of grain in the garrison was soon exhausted, the besieged must have been compelled to surrender; * * * The divisions on the west and south faces erected batteries, but a grand attack was directed against the North-East angle which assumes nearly the shape of a tower and is one of the strongest points, the rock being forty-two feet high, and the bastion, now on the top of it, consists of twenty-five feet of masonry, making a total height of sixty-seven feet. Turbeeut Khān undertook to mine this angle and at the end of four months and a half had completed two mines. So confident were the Moghuls of success that the storming party was ready formed but concealed, as much as possible, under the brow of the hill from the view of the garrison. Aurungzebe was invited to view the spectacle, and a stratagem was formed to draw all the garrison towards the bastion, by the Emperor's moving off from that side in grand procession, so that when the match was ready to be applied, hundreds of Mahrāttās, attracted by his splendid retinue, crowded to the rampart, among others Prayāgjee the commandant. The first mine was fired, it burst several fissures in the rock, and occasioned so violent a concussion, that a great part of the masonry was thrown inwards, and crushed many of the garrison in its ruins. The storming party, in their eagerness, advanced nearer, the match was applied to the train of the second and larger mine, but being improperly constructed, it burst outwards with a dreadful explosion and upwards of two thousand of the Moghuls are said to have been destroyed on the spot. Prayāgji, the Mahrātta commandant, wa buried in the ruins by the first explosion, close to a temple dedicated to the goddess Bhowānee, but was afterwards dug out alive. His escape was considered a happy omen and under other circumstances might have been of much consequence in animating the Hindu garrison to prolong the defence. * * Satara surrendered about the middle of April, 1700."[1]

Sindia.

"The result left Sindia all-powerful in Hindoostan, but he was conscious of his unpopularity in the Deccan, and strove to overcome it. With this view he had, on his arrival at Poona, espoused the cause of Govind Rāo Gāekwār in a manner which will be hereafter explained."[2]

Sitārām Rāvji.

"Having previously adopted his nephew Seetārām Rowjee as his son, he was, with the consent of the resident, appointed successor (to Rowji Appāji)."[3]

---

[1] Grant Duff, Vol. I, pp. 393-4.
[2] Grant Duff, Vol. I, p. 84.
[3] Grant Duff, Vol. III, p. 367.

INDEX AND GLOSSARY.

C

Samsthānik—One that enjoys a royal city or town made over to him for his maintenance.

Samvat—The era of Vikramāditya.

Sanad—A sealed paper of authority commanding, authorizing, appointing or granting free-holds.

Sardārship—The office or duty of a *Sardār*, chiefship, rule, etc.

Sardeshmukhi—A levy from tne *Rayyets* of ten rupees for every hundred levied by the Government.

T

U

V

W

Y

Auranjeb.

C. S. Press, Poona.

Babaji Appaji, Minister of Baroda (Conqueror of Kathiawar).

Bajirav II.-the last of the Peshvas.

C. S. Press, Poona.

Bapu Gokhale.

C. S. Press, Poona.

Chhatrapati Shivaji.

C, S, Press, Poona.

Fattesing Gāikvād Sena Khāskel Samsher Bahādar.

General Sakharam Hari Gupte.

Haripant Fadake.

C. S. Press, Poona.

MADHAJI SCINDE (Conqueror of Delhi).

Minister Rāvji Appaji's Marble Cenotaph

Nana Fadanavis.

C. S. Press, Poona.

Raghunathrav Peshva (Raghoba Dada.)

C. S. Press, Poona.

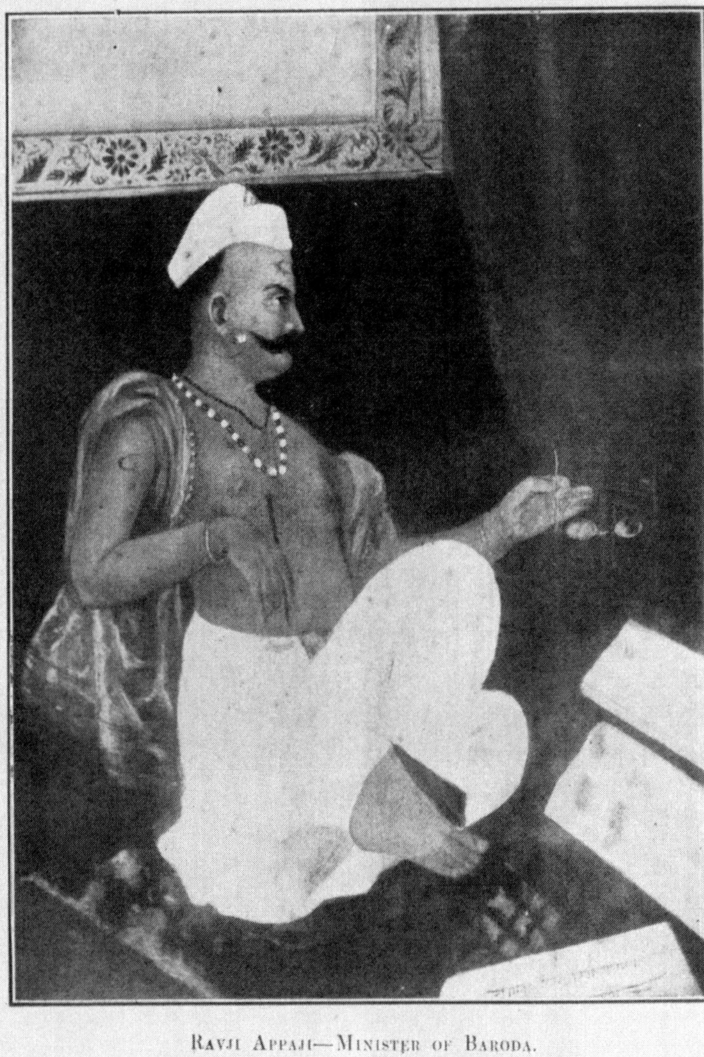

Ravji Appaji—Minister of Baroda.

Shahu Chhatrapati (Shivaji II.)

C. S. Press, Poona.

Shrimant Narayanrav Peshva.

C. S. Press, Poona.

SENA-KHĀSKEL-SAMSHER-BAHĀDAR GANPATRAO GAIKWAD OF BARODA.

Shri. Savai Madhavrav Peshva.

C. S. Press, Poona.